THE
LIVING ROOM

by

GRAHAM GREENE

With an Introduction by
PETER GLENVILLE

HEINEMANN

LONDON

Heinemann Educational Books Ltd
LONDON EDINBURGH MELBOURNE TORONTO
SINGAPORE JOHANNESBURG HONG KONG
NAIROBI AUCKLAND IBADAN
NEW DELHI

ISBN 0 435 20360 6

Acknowledgements are due to Mr. Roy Campbell for permission to use at the beginning of Act II a passage from his translation of "The Poems of St. John of the Cross" (Harvill Press)

FIRST PUBLISHED 1953
FIRST PUBLISHED IN THE DRAMA LIBRARY 1955
REPRINTED 1957, 1960, 1964, 1968, 1971

PUBLISHED BY
HEINEMANN EDUCATIONAL BOOKS LTD
48 CHARLES STREET, LONDON W1X 8AH
PRINTED OFFSET LITHO AND BOUND IN GREAT BRITAIN
BY COX & WYMAN LTD
LONDON, FAKENHAM AND READING

16391

THE DRAMA LIBRARY

General Editor—Edward Thompson

To

CATHERINE WITH LOVE

CHARACTERS

MARY (the daily woman)
MICHAEL DENNIS
ROSE PEMBERTON
MISS TERESA BROWNE
MISS HELEN BROWNE
FATHER JAMES BROWNE
MRS. DENNIS

SCENES

ACT ONE

SCENE I.   The Living Room.   An afternoon in January.
SCENE II.   The same.   The next morning.

ACT TWO

SCENE I.   The Living Room.   Three weeks later.
                    Late afternoon.
SCENE II.   The same.   The next morning.

THE LIVING ROOM, was first presented on Thursday, 16 April, 1953, at Wyndham's Theatre, London. With the following cast:

MARY	Dorothy Dewhurst
MICHAEL DENNIS	John Robinson
ROSE PEMBERTON	Dorothy Tutin
MISS TERESA BROWNE	Mary Jerrold
MISS HELEN BROWNE	Violet Farebrother
FATHER JAMES BROWNE	Eric Portman
MRS. DENNIS	Valerie Taylor

The Play directed by
PETER GLENVILLE

with Settings by
LESLIE HURRY

INTRODUCTION

by

PETER GLENVILLE

THE LIVING ROOM is a difficult play, difficult and unexpected both in theme and manner. It is full of mood and challenge; elusive and yet passionate with conviction. All major artists create their own personal and individual world; a world informed by their own outlook and vision. Recently promoters of plays and films have tried to escape from the problem and responsibility of finding new creative writers by evolving what is known as the documentary style. Plays and films of this kind are not without interest in their dispassionate account of the world of facts and figures in which we live, but they belong to the world of journalism rather than to that of dramatic literature. The writings of Graham Greene appear to have the salty detailed immediacy of actual everyday life, but in fact it is everyday life brilliantly transformed by Mr. Greene's special imagination and personality. This is also true of his play, *The Living Room*, and consequently the cast, director, and designer of the play must understand and evoke this ambiance in order to interpret it successfully. The vocabulary of Graham Greene's thought and mood is sharply defined, inelastic. It borrows nothing from stock theatrical convention. The style and rhythm have to be discovered freshly by the producer and by the actors. It must depend on a rigid economy of method and a close imaginative concentration on essentials of character. Even the most tasteful devices by which actors can magnetize, beguile, or charm their audiences must be discarded for this play. Theatricality or falseness of any kind will seem out of place and will inevitably cause laughter. The febrility and high tension of the writing requires the utmost simplicity and truth in the playing. There is no compromise here with romantic make believe, with glamour, or with good-natured charm. The characters are shown as poor bare forked animals, unaccommodated by allure or camouflage, and if they are to live happily ever after, it certainly won't be this side of the Styx.

The majority of modern English plays are romantically conceived, and their absence of intellectual vitality is compensated for by a warm optimism in the emotional pattern. In this play there is a firm and masculine optimism in the matter of intellectual conviction, combined with a searing pessimism about anything that concerns the question of immediate satisfaction of emotional needs. Moreover it is written within the framework and premise of Catholic belief. This play is no apologia for Catholicism. Indeed the particular Catholics with whom it deals are shown as being misguided, uncomprehending, unhappy, and with their backs to the wall. The play is not for or against Catholics, it is about them—or rather about certain individual Catholics who find themselves (through their own fault) in a terrible dilemma; a dilemma pushed to its farthest limit. This, it could be argued, is a necessary condition of any good play, be it tragedy or farce.

The cast and director should not concern themselves with the pros and cons regarding Catholic belief. They should concentrate on understanding the characters within the framework and story of the play, and on absorbing the style and mood in which it is written.

Michael Dennis is in some ways the most difficult part to play. He enters at once with Rose, tired, and bitter with the guilt of having seduced an orphan girl in his charge at an overnight hotel; he is unhappy and strained with physical desire for her, and yet sincere and pitiable, and not at all lacking in integrity. All this must be suggested within the first few moments they are on the stage alone together. Both he and Rose must suggest the pain of physical longing; a longing and a love which Dennis realises holds little hope of happiness for either of them. For him this love can have no gaiety, and Rose is soon to learn that for her it can have no resolution. At the end of the play he is left protesting bleakly; and she is dead; "A stone in a pond."

In the casting of the play it is as well to remember that the story has no villain. The two foolish old women who do not understand the essentials of their own religion, must be sympathetically understandable. Helen, who precipitates the tragedy because of her lack of charity, is herself the unhappy victim of fear; and she sincerely believes that she is right in all her actions. If Helen is played as a woman impelled by actively evil motives, the situation and plot will degenerate into melodrama. The only evil in Helen is an absence of a sufficiency of good. She wishes to act rightly but her charity is not large enough to know what right is. She is incomplete, stupid even, but never wicked in the romantic sense of the word. In physical type it is advisable to cast an actress who is large, healthy and jolly-looking. An angular actress who specialises in playing melodramatic roles of a villanous kind could ruin the proper performance of the play. The choice of actress for this part is one of the most crucial decisions the director will have to make.

James, the crippled priest, requires an actor of great inner strength and simplicity. He is no intellectual, but at the same time he has to justify the underlying religious premises of the play; and he can only do so by suggesting the workings of the man's mind, which, although limited, is strong. "My senses don't feel it," he says about his faith, "they feel nothing but revolt, uncertainty, despair—but I know it at the back of my mind." As a priest he fails Rose in her moment of crisis, and as a man he feels the full weight of remorse and guilt; yet in the pungent and daring last scene he justifies, not himself, for that he cannot do, but the idea to which he adheres in spite of all, that behind the preceding tragic events can be seen the workings of a benevolent God.

To achieve a décor that is exactly right for the play is more difficult than might appear to the casual reader. As a living room it must seem odd and wrong. It is a room unusual in itself and it is being used for purposes foreign to its shape and character. At the same time it should be effective and atmospheric as a setting, and it must also afford adequate opportunities for the necessary movement and action of the play. Scenery is always scenery, however deceptively real it may appear. There are many ways for a scenic artist to suggest this reality. However, it is difficult for him to design a room that does not have the appearance of a proper room at all, to indicate in fact that everything about it looks all wrong without running the risk that as a set his design itself will look all wrong; and that it does not have the proper appearance of a living room because it is not a room at all but just a theatre setting. The opening lines of the dialogue refer to the room. "What an odd room! It's the wrong shape. Do you see what I mean? Nothing quite fits," says Michael; and what he says could easily be thought to apply to an indifferent job of designing on the part of the artist. Another difficulty is that the corridor and stairs have to be indicated, and, at certain moments, they should be actually seen. Leslie Hurry, whose décor for the play in my opinion was exceptional, solved this problem by making one side of the room transparent when occasion demanded that we should see outside of it on to the landing and stairs. This convention was open to criticism on the grounds of being contrary to the logic of the rest of the room which remained opaque, but it did allow the audience to see the action outside. Of course a divided set could have been devised, but this would hardly have been justified in view of the small amount of action that took place in this outside area.

There is no conventional theatrical style upon which to fall back for the performance of this play. Graham Greene creates his own special music and his interpreters must have an ear for it. It is a music that is direct, occasionally discordant, and always virile.

ACT I

SCENE I

The Living Room. An afternoon in January.

At first sight, when the curtain rises, we are aware of something strange about the living-room. The house is an ordinary Holland Park house, and there is nothing at first on which we can positively lay a finger and say, 'this is wrong', or 'this is strange'. Through a tall window at the back we see only the tops of the trees outside and the window is oddly barred up half its height. Is it that the furniture—in a fashion difficult to define—doesn't quite fit, as though it had been chosen for a larger room of a different shape? But there are many explanations for that in these days. There are two doors to the room—one is open on to the landing, the other up a small flight of stairs is closed. As the curtain rises, a bell downstairs is ringing.

MARY comes rapidly in. She is un-uniformed and you could not believe that those heavy, shapeless legs could belong to anyone less independent than a daily woman. She mounts the stairs to the closed door and turns the handle. It is locked.

MARY (*softly*): Miss Teresa . . .

She listens for a moment, and then as the bell rings again, goes out to the landing and we hear her rattling down the stairs.

Almost at the same moment we hear the sound of water pouring away from a basin in a closet, behind the second door. That for a moment seems to focus the oddness, the uneasiness of this room, for who would expect a lavatory to open immediately out of a living-room as though it were—perhaps we are now reaching the heart of the problem—really a bedroom? Voices mount the stairs—a man's voice and MARY's.

MARY: Miss Browne will be glad to see you here, Miss Rose, safe and sound.

MICHAEL: I hope she got my wire. Phew! This has been quite a climb.

MARY: It's warm for the time of year, sir.

MICHAEL: Is it? Not in the train. The heating wasn't on.

MARY shows in MICHAEL DENNIS, a man in the middle forties with a strained, rather sullen face anxious about too many things and too anxious to disguise his anxiety, and ROSE PEMBERTON, a girl of about twenty with a look of being not quite awake, a bewildered tousled-pillow face, a face which depends for its prettiness on youth. It will never again be quite so pretty as this year—or even this month.

MARY: Miss Browne will be down in a minute, sir.

She goes out.

MICHAEL: Down? She must live in an attic.

MICHAEL and ROSE stand stiffly, a little apart, looking round the room.

Why have a living-room on the third floor? Do you think it's to discourage callers? (*He moves restlessly around, but comes back to exactly the same spot, three feet away from the girl.*) What an odd room! It's the wrong shape. Do you see what I mean? Nothing quite fits. I wonder where that goes to? (*He indicates the stairs to the closet door, climbs them, and tries the handle. He returns to the same spot of carpet.*) The Browne family's skeleton? Browne with an E. Haven't you anything to say? Some joke? Something to show that we don't really care a damn?

ROSE shakes her head.

Well, I've delivered you safely. The reliable family friend. You are only twelve hours late. And we sent the right considerate telegram. The orphan is safe. But they wouldn't have worried. You were in *my* hands.

ROSE puts out a hand and touches him. He puts his hand over hers, holding it tightly, but they keep the same distance.

Be careful! You can always trust me to be very careful. I've reached the careful age. Wasn't my planning perfect? The two rooms at opposite ends of the corridor. And even the

Boots was not up when our alarm went. The shoes stood on parade all down the corridor—in the correct positions.

ROSE (*imploringly*): Do you have to? Isn't it bad enough, darling?——

MICHAEL: Careful, again. Darling is a word we mustn't use. Perhaps 'dear' would be all right, from a man of my age. A safely married man. But when I say dear, remember it means—just that. Dear.

ROSE: We can hear anybody coming up the stairs.

She kisses him, and at that moment a key turns in the closet door. They leap to their original positions as the door opens and MISS TERESA BROWNE comes out—an old lady who must have passed seventy a long while ago. She closes the door behind her.

Aunt Helen . . .

TERESA BROWNE pays not the slightest attention. She walks by them as though they were not there and out through the door on to the landing.

MICHAEL: Why did she go out like that? Why didn't she speak? Do you think she saw us?

ROSE: No. Perhaps she heard something.

MICHAEL: There wasn't much to hear.

TERESA re-enters. She holds out her hand and smiles with restrained cordiality.

TERESA: My dear, you must be Rose. Mary never told me you'd arrived.

ROSE (*kissing her*): And you are Aunt Helen. Or do I have to call you Great-Aunt?

TERESA: I'm Aunt Teresa, dear.

ROSE: How silly of me!

TERESA: Not silly after all these years. You were only six, weren't you?

ROSE: Only six. This is Mr. Dennis, Aunt Teresa.

TERESA: I'm interested to meet you, Mr. Dennis. My poor niece mentioned you often in her letters.

ROSE (*to MICHAEL*): My mother.

3

MICHAEL: Of course. I hope you don't think, Miss Browne, that I've let down your trust already.

TERESA: I don't know what you mean, Mr. Dennis. Trust?

MICHAEL: We're twelve hours late. It seemed sensible to catch an early morning train instead of travelling after the funeral.

TERESA: I was sorry not to be there, dear. But I couldn't leave your uncle and your Aunt Helen. You found a room in the village, I hope, Mr. Dennis?

MICHAEL: Oh, yes. The Red Lion.

TERESA: Mass was said for your mother this morning, dear, by Father Turner.

ROSE: Oh, I'm sorry. I didn't know. I should have been there.

TERESA: We were all there—even my brother—we remembered you with her. Are you a Catholic, Mr. Dennis?

MICHAEL (*abruptly*): No.

TERESA: How odd that my niece should have left you her executor.

ROSE (*with asperity*): Why not? My father wasn't a Catholic.

TERESA: No, dear. Poor man. Would you like a cup of tea, Mr. Dennis?

MICHAEL: You mustn't bother. I only came to hand over Rose . . .

TERESA: A labourer deserves his hire. Excuse me a moment, Mr. Dennis.

She goes to the door and calls 'Mary!' No answer. She goes out on to the landing and calls again 'Mary'.

(*From the landing*). What time is it, Mr. Dennis?

MICHAEL: Just gone five.

TERESA: Mary always leaves so punctually, but she's paid till five-fifteen.

MICHAEL: I've really got to go.

TERESA: My brother always likes his cup. Mary!

She goes downstairs.

4

MICHAEL: Well, we've broken the ice. That's not a good phrase, is it, for a pair of people skating like we are.

ROSE: Darling, what are you worrying about? Me? You don't have to. I swear it. (*With a touch of bitterness.*) I loved you the night of my mother's funeral. That's an oath, isn't it, like mixing blood. For ever and ever. Amen.

MICHAEL: Oh, it's myself I'm worrying about. I'm afraid you're going to disappear. In a wood of old people. I'm afraid I'm losing you—the minutes are hurrying. What happens tomorrow?

> *He moves around the room while she stays still, at a loss, in the centre of it.*

ROSE: You don't have to worry—You can't lose me. After all, you're the executer.

MICHAEL: You mean the executor, yes, I suppose I can always see you on business. (*Mounting the stairs.*) She came from up here. (*He opens the closet door.*) It just doesn't make sense. The third floor. A bathroom out of the sitting-room. This must have been a bedroom.

> MISS HELEN BROWNE *enters.*

HELEN: You're Rose?

> *They kiss.*

My dear little sweetheart, I used to call you. And you are Mr. Dennis?

> *They shake hands.*

Oh, you wouldn't believe what a bad little sweetheart she could be sometimes.

> *She is a little younger than her sister—a fat woman, with a certain bonhomie. She can steer straight through other people's lives without noticing.*

Teresa told me you'd arrived. She's making tea. The maid left too early, but the clock in the kitchen's fast. Rose, dear, perhaps you'd give her a hand with the bread-and-butter.

ROSE: I'm afraid I don't know where . . .

HELEN: Straight down the stairs and into the basement. You'll hear her cluttering around. (*To* MICHAEL.) My poor sister's eyesight's failing. It's to be expected, of course, at seventy-eight.

ROSE (*to* MICHAEL): I'll see you . . .?

HELEN: Mr. Dennis will stay to tea, won't you, Mr. Dennis?

ROSE *leaves the room—unwillingly.*

I was so sorry not to have been at the church. But you do understand, don't you, I couldn't leave my brother and sister. Do sit down.

MICHAEL: I hadn't meant to stay.

HELEN: Oh, but there's so much we would like to hear. (*She sits firmly down in the most comfortable chair.*) The Brownes all have long ears, like the Flopsy Bunnies. You know the Flopsy Bunnies, Mr. Dennis?

MICHAEL: I don't think I do.

HELEN: Not dear Beatrix Potter? But, of course, she was my generation. I saw her once shopping at Debenham's. Now I'd expected you—somehow—to be an older man.

MICHAEL: I'm forty-five. (*He sits unwillingly.*)

HELEN: Catholics are much too clanny sometimes, don't you think? Dear Teresa was quite surprised when my niece chose someone who wasn't a Catholic as a trustee.

MICHAEL: I was her husband's friend, you know—his pupil, too. I owe everything to him. Even my job now—at London University.

HELEN: You'll think us rather bigoted, but we never cared very much for poor John's profession. It would have been so awkward for my niece if it had been—condemned.

MICHAEL: I'm afraid you won't approve of my profession then—but I'm a mere *lecturer* in psychology. Not a professor.

HELEN: Oh well, of course, it doesn't matter about you, does it, Mr. Dennis? We aren't concerned. And the will? We've had no details yet. (*Coyly.*) Long ears again.

MICHAEL: Rose will have about eight hundred a year of

her own at the age of twenty-five. Until then, your brother and I are trustees.

HELEN: It might have been better to have kept it in the family instead of troubling you. (*Coyly*.) Now I'm being clanny too.

MICHAEL: You see, her father appointed me a trustee before he died, and Mrs. Pemberton just let it stand. His friends were always her friends. I used to visit them every summer after his death.

HELEN (*sadly*): She was the first Browne to marry a non-Catholic.

MICHAEL (*with a smile*): The first Browne?

HELEN: The first of *our* Brownes. And you are the executor too, Mr. Dennis?

MICHAEL: As I was trustee I suppose the lawyers thought it would make things go more smoothly. I shall resign as trustee as soon as the will's executed. You'll be free of me.

HELEN: Oh, but of course I didn't mean . . .

MICHAEL: I don't think I'm quite made to be a trustee, Miss Browne.

HELEN (*almost as though she had taken his point*): We *were* a little anxious about Rose until we got your telegram.

MICHAEL: She was tired by the funeral. It would have been too much to travel all night. I thought the day train——

HELEN: Poor Rose—it must have been lonely in that house all by herself.

MICHAEL: Better than travelling, of course. (*Explaining a little too much*.) I got a room at the Red Lion for myself.

HELEN: So right of you, Mr. Dennis. In a village like that there'd have been a lot of silly talk if you'd stayed in the house.

MICHAEL: Even about a man of my age and a girl of hers?

HELEN (*cheerfully and inexorably*): Human nature's such a terrible thing, Mr. Dennis. Or is that very Roman of me?

MICHAEL: I haven't found it terrible. Complicated, tangled, perhaps unhappy. Needing help.

HELEN: My niece wrote in one of her last letters that you had been very helpful. We are so grateful for that. There was little we could do.

She notices that MICHAEL *is a little absent. The room still puzzles him. He cannot help looking here and there, particularly at the stains on the wall.*

(*Making conversation*). But now we can all help Rose to forget.

MICHAEL: I'm very sorry. What was that? Forget?

HELEN: Her dear mother.

MICHAEL: Is it always a good thing to forget? Of course my job is usually to teach people the importance of remembering.

HELEN: What are you staring at, Mr. Dennis?

MICHAEL: Was I staring?

HELEN: I'm afraid it *is* rather a cluttered room. But you see, it's our only living-room.

MICHAEL: It looks quite a big house from outside.

HELEN: A great many of the rooms are closed.

MICHAEL: War damage?

HELEN (*guardedly*): For one reason or another.

As he still looks around.

All the rooms need repapering, but one doesn't like to spend capital, does one?

Teresa enters, carrying a cake-stand with bread-and-butter on one level and a plum cake on another.

TERESA: The kettle's boiling, Helen. We shan't be a moment, Mr. Dennis. Everything's set.

In this household she is obviously the anxious Martha; the weaker character intent on carrying out orders. The orders are first thought up somewhere else, presumably behind that mask of bonhomie her slightly younger sister presents to the world.

MICHAEL: It's good of you, but I hadn't meant to stay.

TERESA: Oh, but you must meet our brother.

HELEN: Don't press Mr. Dennis, Teresa. He may have all sorts of things . . .

8

MICHAEL: Perhaps I ought to have a word with—your niece, before I go.

TERESA: With my niece? But she's . . . she's . . . dead.

HELEN (*sharply*): He means Rose, dear.

MICHAEL: There's still a lot of business to be done. About the will. You see, the other executor is abroad.

TERESA: What a good thing you're a careful man, Mr. Dennis!

MICHAEL: Am I careful?

TERESA: That's what you were telling Rose, wasn't it? 'You can always trust me,' you said, 'to be very careful.' I thought it was so sweetly put.

MICHAEL (*covering up*): Well, an executor has to be careful—or he goes to jail.

HELEN (*defining his sphere of interest*): You should really see my brother about all those legal things. Rose is too young to understand. Dear little sweetheart! Teresa, if Rose is tired, tell her to lie down. We can entertain Mr. Dennis.

ROSE *returns on that word, carrying the tea-things.*

ROSE: I'm not a bit tired.

HELEN: Well then, if you'll all sit down (do take off your coat, Mr. Dennis), I'll push James in. (You know he's been confined to his chair for years.) Start pouring out the tea, dear.

She goes out.

TERESA (*fussing with the tea-things*): Now find yourselves chairs. No, not that one, Rose. That's your Aunt Helen's.

ROSE *and* MICHAEL *sit down together. They don't look at each other. Constraint keeps their eyes on a mutual object, as if it is only there, where* TERESA *deals with the tea-things, that their gaze can meet vicariously.*

Where did you say you went to Mass today, dear?

ROSE: I didn't, Aunt Teresa.

TERESA: But it's a Holiday of Obligation, dear. Oh well, perhaps it doesn't matter if you were travelling.

ROSE: I forgot. I could have gone before the early train. But I slept so sound.

TERESA: One lump, Mr. Dennis?

MICHAEL: Thank you.

TERESA: And you, Rose?

ROSE: Yes, please, Aunt.

TERESA *is pouring out the tea as she talks.*

TERESA: I started a novena for you as soon as I heard of your poor mother.

ROSE: Thank you, Aunt Teresa.

TERESA: I expect you'd like to go to Mass tomorrow. It's the second of nine we've arranged for her. Mary doesn't come in till eight-thirty, but we'll wake you ourselves.

ROSE: Thank you.

TERESA: Help yourself to bread-and-butter, Mr. Dennis.

ROSE *and* MICHAEL *both put out their hands, touch each other and recoil over the plate.*

(*To* ROSE) Has Helen told you about your room?

ROSE: No, but there's no hurry.

TERESA: You see, dear, we are very cramped for space here. So many rooms are closed. We thought perhaps you wouldn't mind sleeping in here. The sofa's very comfortable. And the end lets down.

ROSE: Of course. I don't mind.

MICHAEL: I was saying to your sister, Miss Browne, that it seemed quite a large house from the street.

TERESA: Oh, it was. It was. But many rooms had to be closed.

MICHAEL: War damage?

TERESA: Not exactly.

HELEN (*outside*): Here we are! Will somebody open the door?

HELEN *pushes in a chair in which sits her brother,* JAMES BROWNE, *a man of about 65, with a face to which one is not sure whether nature or mutilation has lent strength. All his vitality perhaps has had to find its way above the waist. A shawl is over his legs, and he wears a scarf round his neck.*

(*To* JAMES) James, here is Rose—and Mr. Dennis, the executor.

JAMES: It's good to see you, my dear. After all these years. You've changed more than I have.

ROSE *bends down and kisses him.*

ROSE: How are you, Uncle?

JAMES: Pretty well, my dear. Thank God you won't play trains with my chair now! Well, Mr. Dennis, I hope she hasn't been a trouble to you. We expected you last night.

MICHAEL: The morning train seemed a better idea, Mr. Browne.

HELEN: *Father* Browne, Mr. Dennis. My brother's . . .

MICHAEL: Of course. I'm sorry.

JAMES: Now you've seen all the family again, can you bear us, Rose? We are a bit older than we were, but we aren't so bad.

ROSE: It was good of Mother to leave me to you. I'd have been lost without you.

JAMES: The only Catholic Pemberton. But somehow I never think of you as a Pemberton.

TERESA (*handing* JAMES *a cup*): Your tea, dear.

ROSE: Some bread-and-butter, Uncle?

JAMES: No, thank you, dear. Just the tea. I'm not an eating man.

TERESA: Oh, Rose! Such a funny thing happened last night! A lady rang up and she asked if we were the Brownes who were expecting a niece.

ROSE: Who was she?

TERESA: I've no idea. When I told her you weren't arriving till today she just rang off.

HELEN: You never told me, Teresa. What a secret little thing you are!

TERESA: I've only just remembered. (*To* ROSE.) I expect it was a friend of yours who wanted to enquire.

ROSE: I can't think of anybody—in London. (*She looks at* MICHAEL *with apprehension.*)

TERESA: Oh, if it's anything important, I expect she'll ring again. Talking of important, James, Mary left a quarter of an hour early today.

HELEN: It wasn't her fault. The clock in the kitchen is always twenty minutes fast.

> *While the old people talk*, ROSE *and* MICHAEL *sit awkwardly together, saying nothing. They have no small-talk for each other.*

TERESA: Since it's always fast she must know the real time. Will you speak to her, James? She would take it better from you. Oh ... (*Putting her cup suddenly down, she makes for the door.*)

HELEN: Now, dear, what is it?

TERESA: If Mary left early, I don't know how the oven is.

HELEN: It can wait for a few minutes. What a little Martha you are!

TERESA: You'd be the first to complain tonight about the pie.

HELEN: Well then, let me go, dear, and I'll have only myself to blame.

TERESA: The cooking tonight is *my* responsibility. Isn't that so, James?

JAMES: It's a Thursday. Yes.

HELEN: I'll help you, dear. I can't bear to see you lifting heavy things.

> *During the argument* ROSE *and* MICHAEL *have drawn a little apart from the others.*

> TERESA *leaves the room.*

> HELEN *is about to follow her when she looks round and sees* MICHAEL'S *hand touching* ROSE'S *as he takes her empty cup.*

ROSE: Thank you, dear. (*She tries to swallow the last word, but it's too late.*)

HELEN: See that Mr. Dennis has a slice of my plum cake, James.

> *She leaves.*

JAMES: She has a wonderful hand with cakes, Mr. Dennis.

MICHAEL: I don't think I will. I ought to be going home.

ROSE: I'm sorry.

MICHAEL: Why?

ROSE: I mean, I've been such a trouble.

MICHAEL: No trouble. But my wife gets anxious rather easily. She's—not very well. I should have gone straight home, but I thought there were things we ought to discuss—about the will.

ROSE (*anxious to ensure seeing her lover the next day*): No, no. It can wait. Till tomorrow. You'll be coming in tomorrow? We can talk then.

MICHAEL: Of course. Any time that suits you. I'll ring you up in the morning. Have a good rest tonight.

> *They are trying to reassure each other in* FATHER BROWNE'S *presence.*

ROSE: You've done so much for me.

MICHAEL: It's my job. I'm the executor—not the exec*u*ter.

ROSE: It was a silly slip. I was never much good at English.

MICHAEL: As the executor and trustee (*slowly and firmly*) I'll try not to make any slips at all. Good-bye, Father Browne.

JAMES: Good-bye, Mr. Dennis. We'll be seeing each other again soon, I hope.

ROSE: You put some papers down . . . over there, I think.

> *It is an excuse for them to move behind the old man's chair, out of his vision. They are afraid to kiss, but they hold each other for a moment.*

MICHAEL: They must be in my overcoat pocket.

> *They go together to the door.*

Don't come down. It's a long way to the hall. I'll see you tomorrow, Rose.

ROSE: Yes.

MICHAEL (*with a last look at this room which is the wrong shape*): Good-bye.

> *He goes.*

ROSE *follows him on to the landing. We can hear his steps on the stairs, but she still doesn't return. A pause.*

JAMES: Come in, dear, and have another cup of tea.

ROSE (*returning*): I don't awfully like tea.

JAMES (*guessing her thoughts*): Yes, it's a long way down, isn't it? Only the kitchen is in the place you'd expect. In the basement. Even if you don't like tea, come in and sit down. I don't see many strangers.

ROSE: Am I a stranger?

JAMES: One can love a stranger.

ROSE: Yes. (*She comes back, but her mind is away.*) Why are so many rooms closed, Uncle?

JAMES: Have you noticed? So quickly?

ROSE: I mistook the floor just now—it's a strange house— the rooms down there seemed locked.

JAMES: I suppose I ought to tell you. But it comes from something very foolish.

ROSE: Yes?

JAMES: I wouldn't tell you if you were just staying a while. But this has got to be your home. You'll see it for yourself. You'll watch your Aunt Teresa . . . your Aunt Helen, and I suppose there's a lot to puzzle you.

ROSE: I thought it was funny the way Aunt Teresa came out of there, not paying any attention . . .

JAMES: Yes, it's funny, isn't it? Go on thinking it's funny— a bit pathetic, too. There's no harm in it. Don't let it get on your nerves. I sometimes think the young have worse nerves than we have. Age is a good drug and it doesn't lose its effect.

ROSE: But you still haven't told me.

JAMES: My dear, it's so absurd! And I should have been able to stop it. I hope you'll laugh. Please laugh—it's very funny—in its way.

ROSE: Yes?

JAMES (*nerving himself*): You see, your Aunt Helen sleeps in the old drawing-room. Because I'm an invalid they would

14

have insisted on the dining-room for me, but I told them they couldn't get me up and down stairs to the living-room, so I have what used to be a nurse's little sitting-room here—by the night nursery—this was the night nursery in the old days. Aunt Teresa has the day nursery next to me. You see the bedrooms are all closed.

ROSE: But why?

JAMES (*slowly and reluctantly*): They don't like using a room in which anybody has ever died.

ROSE (*not understanding*): Died?

JAMES (*purposely light*): It's a habit people have—in bed-rooms. So the bedrooms are all shut up—except this. It's an old house, and they aren't taking any chances. They risked this one—it had been a night nursery for a long time, and children don't die very often. Anyway, they don't die of old age.

ROSE: When did it all start?

JAMES: I'm not sure. I only noticed it when our father died. It had seemed quite natural when my mother's room was shut; there was nobody else to sleep in it. I only came for the holidays, and they had no visitors. But when this (*he taps his leg*) happened and I came to live here, I noticed our father's room was closed too, and when I wanted a room on the second floor Teresa said—I think it was Teresa—'but that was Rose's room'.

ROSE: Rose?

JAMES: Your grandmother. She was the only one of us who got married. She died here, you know, when your mother was born.

ROSE: Was that when it started?

JAMES: It may have been. Who knows when anything really starts? Perhaps it was when we were all children to-gether in this room.

A pause.

ROSE: It's—creepy, isn't it?

JAMES: No, no, my dear. Not creepy. I used to laugh at them and threaten to die in here. What will you do for a living-room then? I'd say. But I think at the last moment they'd push me into my own room—and that could be closed afterwards.

ROSE: But I still don't understand.

JAMES: Nor do I. Perhaps it's the fear of death—of the certainty of death. They don't seriously mind accidents. They aren't so much worried about your poor mother—because she was still young. She needn't have died. It's the inevitable they hate. Of course when someone dies they'll do all the right things—they are good Catholics. They'll have Masses said—and then as quickly as possible they forget. The photographs are the first things to disappear.

ROSE: But why? why?

JAMES: You'll have to ask Dennis. He lectures and writes books and teaches psychology. I expect he'd call it an anxiety neurosis. Or something more difficult. I'm a priest and I've given up psychology. They are good people, I doubt if they've ever committed a big sin in their lives—perhaps it would have been better if they had. I used to notice, in the old days, it was often the sinners who had the biggest trust. In mercy. My sisters don't seem to have any trust. Are you afraid of death?

ROSE: I don't think so. I haven't thought.

JAMES: Of course it seems closer to them than to you.

ROSE: Are you afraid of it, Uncle?

JAMES: I used to be—twenty years ago. And then something worse happened to me. It was like God reproving me for being such a fool. When that car smash came I ceased to be any use. I am a priest who can't say Mass or hear confessions or visit the sick. I shouldn't have been afraid of dying. I should have been afraid of being useless.

ROSE: But you *are* of use to them, Uncle?

JAMES: A priest isn't intended to be just a comfort to his

16

family. Sometimes in the morning when I am half asleep, I imagine my legs are still here. I say to myself, Oh dear, oh dear, what a day ahead! A meeting of the Knights of Saint Columba, and then the Guild of the Blessed Sacrament, a meeting of the Altar Society, and after that . . . It's strange how bored I used to be with all the running around.

ROSE: Now I'm here, can't we go out together to the river and the park?

JAMES: Yes. I'd like to now and then. But it means hiring a couple of men. It's a long way down the stairs, and I'm heavy. But I'm not going to use you, my dear. I hope soon you'll be getting married.

ROSE: There's plenty of time.

HELEN *enters.*

HELEN: Poor little fusspot. The oven was perfectly all right. Mary's very reliable. Has Mr. Dennis gone?

JAMES: He went a few minutes ago.

HELEN: A nice man, but not much sense of humour, I'm afraid. I was telling him about the Flopsy Bunnies. He'd never heard of them.

JAMES: You mustn't be hard on him for that. I've never read *Paradise Lost.*

TERESA *enters in a hurry.*

TERESA: Has Mr. Dennis . . .?

HELEN: He's gone, dear.

TERESA: That lady is on the telephone again. The one who called before. She wants to talk to him.

ROSE: I have his number. (*With a trace of bitterness at the last word.*) She can get him at home.

TERESA: I said I thought I'd heard him go, and she wants to talk to you, Rose.

ROSE (*scared*): Me?

TERESA: She says she's Mrs. Dennis. Will you speak to her, dear? She's asking all sorts of questions I can't answer.

ROSE: But I don't know her. I've never even met her.

HELEN *is listening intently.*

JAMES: What questions, Teresa?

TERESA: She said she tried to speak to Mr. Dennis last night. She wasn't well. Where do you say he stayed, dear?

ROSE: I don't know. In the village.

TERESA: And then she tried your house, and you weren't there. She sounds a little—strange. I wish you'd come, dear. She's waiting on the telephone.

JAMES: Better have a word with her.

ROSE (*desperately*): I can't. I don't know her. Michael will be home any moment.

HELEN: Don't worry, my little sweetheart. She's tired. Such a long journey. Your Aunt Helen will take care of it for you.

She leaves.

CURTAIN

SCENE II

The Living Room. The next morning.

MICHAEL DENNIS *is alone. He is ill at ease. He opens a brief-case, takes out some papers and puts them back. He goes to the window and looks out.* TERESA BROWNE *enters.*

TERESA: Good morning, Mr. Dennis.

MICHAEL: Good morning. I promised yesterday I'd come in.

TERESA: We hadn't expected you quite so early.

MICHAEL: I have a lecture at eleven.

TERESA: My brother hasn't finished his breakfast. You see, my sister and I went to Mass this morning.

MICHAEL: I didn't want to bother your brother. It was really Rose I came to see.

TERESA: Oh, but Rose is out. She didn't go to Mass.

MICHAEL: I could come this afternoon. After three. I have some students at two.

TERESA: She's going out this afternoon.

MICHAEL: Well, perhaps I could look in after dinner.

TERESA: She'll be out then—so my sister says.

MICHAEL (*with sombre realisation*): And tomorrow—does Miss Browne say she'll be out then, too?

TERESA: Yes.

MICHAEL: Why?

TERESA: I suppose she knows the reason. I don't.

MICHAEL: Where is Rose?

TERESA: I don't know. I really don't, Mr. Dennis. I'm never told anything in this house.

MICHAEL: I'm the executor of her mother's will—and her trustee. Your sister can't prevent my discussing matters with her.

TERESA: I've no idea what she can do and what she can't, Mr. Dennis. She's a terribly determined woman. I'm her elder, but she's always had her way. Even my brother—and he's a priest. . . . Do you know, Mr. Dennis, she's so arranged this house that . . . that . . . (*Her eyes are on the closet.*) Well, I'm quite ashamed. I don't know what strangers think. We should have made one out of the cupboard on the landing.

MICHAEL: Suppose I just stay here till Rose comes in?

TERESA: Oh, I don't *know* that she's out. And if she's not out, she wouldn't be able to come in, would she?

MICHAEL: Miss Browne, could you take a message . . .

TERESA: I'd have to ask Helen.

MICHAEL: But I'm Rose's trustee.

TERESA: Helen thinks that was a mistake.

MICHAEL (*with anger*): I don't care what Miss Browne thinks . . .

> HELEN *pushes* JAMES *through the door which* TERESA *has left open. She has shed her bonhomie and we can see the strong will buried in the big breasts and the stout body.*

19

HELEN: Good morning, Mr. Dennis. This *is* an early call.

MICHAEL (*stubbornly*): I've come to see Rose. Good morning, Father Browne.

JAMES: I suppose I could make a joke about being pushed into this affair—if it would help.

MICHAEL: It wouldn't. When I don't know what affair . . .

HELEN: Your wife telephoned again, just after you left, Mr. Dennis.

MICHAEL: I know. She told me.

HELEN: Rose is our responsibility now. So you do understand, don't you, we have to clear the matter up.

MICHAEL: What matter?

JAMES: For goodness' sake, sit down, all of you. You make me want to stand up myself.

They prepare to sit.

TERESA: Not that chair, Mr. Dennis. That's Helen's.

HELEN: Teresa dear, don't you think you'd better go and keep an eye on Mary?

TERESA: It's not my turn.

HELEN: I have to have a little talk with Mr. Dennis.

TERESA: But I'm the eldest.

HELEN: That's why, dear. This isn't something for *your* generation.

TERESA (*appealing*): James——?

JAMES: Better go, dear. There are more than enough of us as it is.

HELEN: I heard Mary on the first landing.

TERESA: She's not dusting the closed rooms, is she?

HELEN: I told her particularly not. But perhaps you had better make sure.

TERESA *goes hurriedly out.*

And now, James——

JAMES *sits silent and ill at ease in his wheel-chair. A pause.*
You promised to have a word with Mr. Dennis.

20

JAMES (*with a helpless or perhaps appealing gesture*): Mr. Dennis is not a Catholic. I am not in the confessional. I have no authority.

HELEN: But James, a woman can hardly ask . . .

MICHAEL: This is the second time I've been on trial today. I hope I've reached the Supreme Court. You want to ask me whether Rose and I are lovers. That's it, isn't it?

HELEN: Really, Mr. Dennis, we would never have put it so crudely.

MICHAEL: But I'm not a Catholic, as your brother says. I haven't learned to talk about 'offences against purity'. In my lectures I try to be crude—it's only another word for precise.

JAMES: Forgive me, but so far you haven't been very—precise.

MICHAEL: You said you had no authority. I agree with you. I'm not going to answer.

HELEN: Then we can only assume the worst.

JAMES: Speak for yourself, Helen. I shall do no such thing.

HELEN: Where did you spend the night before last, Mr. Dennis? It wasn't true that you stayed in the village, was it?

MICHAEL: No.

HELEN: Why did you tell us that?

MICHAEL: I *had* booked a room.

HELEN: But when Mrs. Dennis telephoned . . .

MICHAEL: Two people are on trial. I won't answer any questions—unless Rose wants me to. I think you had better let me talk to her.

HELEN: But you won't be able to see her again, Mr. Dennis.

MICHAEL: That's melodramatic and impracticable. (*With sudden fear.*) She's not ill, is she?

JAMES: No.

MICHAEL: You are not dealing with two children, Miss Browne.

HELEN: One is a child.

MICHAEL: Legally, yes, for another year.

HELEN: I agree you are hardly a child. How many children have you, Mr. Dennis?

MICHAEL: None.

HELEN: Why do you want to see Rose again?

MICHAEL: The will . . .

JAMES: Go on being frank. I like you better that way.

MICHAEL (*stung*) I love her. Is that frank enough for you?

HELEN: Frank? It's—it's revolting. Seducing a child at her mother's funeral.

MICHAEL: You take your psychology out of library books, Miss Browne.

HELEN *begins to speak, but* JAMES *interrupts her.*

JAMES: You've asked your questions, Helen. Now leave us alone.

HELEN: Did you hear him admit that . . .

JAMES: There's no point in anger. We only get angry because we are hurt. And our hurt is not of importance in this case. We are dealing with more important people.

HELEN: Are you calling him . . .

JAMES: Of course he's more important than we are. You and I are only capable of *self*-importance, Helen. He's still in the middle of life. He's capable of suffering.

HELEN: I wish you wouldn't preach at me, James.

JAMES: I'm sorry. Sometimes I remember I'm a priest. Please go away.

HELEN: James, will you at least promise . . .

JAMES: Helen, I can't bear your voice when it gets on one note. We are too near death, you and I . . .

HELEN: Oh, you're impossible!

She leaves. A pause.

22

JAMES: I knew that word would do the trick.

MICHAEL: What word?

JAMES: Death.

A pause.

What are we going to do about her?

MICHAEL: Miss Browne seems quite capable . . .

JAMES: I meant Rose. Rose knew you were married?

MICHAEL : Of course.

JAMES: You said this was your second trial today?

MICHAEL *moves restlessly up and down the room, coming to a stop at intervals by the chair.*

MICHAEL: When I got home last night my wife was in bed with the door locked. Like a jury after the evidence has been heard. This morning she gave me her verdict of guilty.

JAMES: Was it a just one?

MICHAEL: Do you believe in justice? (*With angry irony.*) Of course. I forgot. You believe in a just God. The all-wise Judge.

JAMES: That kind of justice has nothing to do with a judge. (*He turns his head and follows* MICHAEL'S *movements.*) It's a mathematical term. We talk of a just line, don't we? God's exact, that's all. He's not a judge. An absolute knowledge of every factor—the conscious and the unconscious—yes, even heredity, all your Freudian urges. That's why He's merciful.

MICHAEL (*coming to a halt by* JAMES'S *chair.*) I know what I seem like to you. I *am* a middle aged man. Whose wife won't divorce him.

JAMES: That wouldn't have helped.

MICHAEL: But I mean to *marry* Rose.

JAMES: It would be better to live with her. She'd be less bound to you then.

MICHAEL: How I hate your logic.

JAMES: I sometimes hate this body cut off at the knees. But my legs won't exist however much I hate the lack of them. It's a waste of time hating facts.

MICHAEL: I believe in different facts.

A pause.

Father, we have our heretics in psychology too. I believe in the analysis of dreams, but sometimes I have had a dream so simple and brief that there seems to be nothing there to analyse—a shape, a few colours, an experience of beauty, that's all. Then I refuse to look further.

JAMES: What has that to do . . .?

MICHAEL: Oh, I can analyse my own love. I can give you all the arguments. Pride that a girl can love me, the idea that time is hurrying to an end, the sense of final vigour which comes before old age, the fascination innocence may have when you've ceased to believe in it—it's like seeing a unicorn in Hyde Park. It's true, Father, you *can* analyse every dream, but sometimes the analysis doesn't seem to make sense. An anxiety neurosis, I say, and then the face stares back at me so young and lovely—why should I explain my love any other way?

JAMES: You don't have to convince a priest that the truth seems all wrong sometimes. I learnt that long ago in the confessional. All the same, I'd rather you were dead. Or somebody different.

MICHAEL: Different?

JAMES: Say, like your grandfather. He may have visited a brothel once in a while, when he went abroad, but he believed you only loved the person you married. He wasn't tempted to leave his wife—society was so strong—any more than you are tempted to commit murder. You may be a better man, but he caused much less trouble.

MICHAEL: It wasn't what I meant to do.

JAMES: You haven't much imagination. How can you have a love affair without trouble?

MICHAEL: I don't want a 'love-affair'. I meant to break it gently to my wife—later, when there wouldn't have been any of this bitterness.

JAMES: I was wrong. You've got a great imagination. If you think you can leave a woman without bitterness.

MICHAEL: My wife and I—we haven't been lovers in a long while.

JAMES: You've been companions, haven't you?

MICHAEL: I didn't mean to hurt anyone. I had planned nothing. I hardly noticed Rose until two months ago. I came to see her mother when the doctors had diagnosed angina. She knew she might die any time, walking too far, lifting a weight. She wanted to talk about Rose. I wasn't a Catholic, but she trusted me. We both lost the man we cared for most when her husband died. Rose came into the room. I didn't bother to look up, but when she bent down to kiss her mother I smelt her hair. Then she went out of the room. She was like a landscape you see from the train, and you want to stop just there.

JAMES: Well?

MICHAEL: I pulled the communication cord.

JAMES: And there's always a fine attached.

MICHAEL: But I want to pay it. Alone. Not the others.

JAMES: Was my sister right? When you went down for the funeral, *were* you planning . . .?

MICHAEL: Not even then. Oh, perhaps I'd be shocked too, if it weren't myself and Rose. You can't shock yourself, can you? 'The funeral bakemeats did coldly furnish forth the marriage tables'. But there hasn't been a marriage. And now there can't be. What do we do?

JAMES: You're the psychologist. Let's hear the wisdom of Freud, Jung, Adler. Haven't they all the answers you need? You can only get a priest's answer from me.

MICHAEL: I'm asking for the priest's answer. Then I'll know what I have to fight.

JAMES: There's only one answer I can give. You're doing wrong to your wife, to Rose, to yourself—and to the God you don't believe in. Go away. Don't see her, don't write to her, don't answer her letters if she writes to you. She'll have a terrible few weeks. So will you. You aren't a cruel man.

MICHAEL: And in the end . . .?

JAMES: We have to trust God. Everything will be all right.

MICHAEL (*angrily*): All right—what a queer idea you have of all right. I've left her. Fine. So she'll always associate love with betrayal. When she loves a man again, there'll always be *that* in her mind . . . love doesn't last. She'll grow her defence mechanisms until she dies inside them. And I'll go on as I have for the last ten years, having a woman now and then, for a night, on the sly, substitutes, living with a woman I don't desire—a hysteric. She has something real for her hysteria now, but for ten years she's invented things. Ever since our child died. Sometimes I find myself thinking she invented even that. I wasn't there.

JAMES: Can't you even find a cure for your own wife?

MICHAEL: No. Because I'm part of her insecurity. I'm inside her neurosis as I'm inside her house.

JAMES: So you'll burn down the house. For God's sake don't talk any more psychology at me. Just tell me what you want.

MICHAEL: To live with Rose. To live an ordinary quiet human life. To have a family. She can change her name to mine for convenience. For the sake of the children. So no one will know. Perhaps one day my wife will divorce me, and we can marry.

JAMES (*ironically*): I shouldn't take the trouble. Rose wouldn't want a fake marriage.

MICHAEL: You don't know her.

JAMES: I know one side of her better than you do. You can't fob off a Catholic with a registrar's signature and call it a marriage. We do as many wrong things as you do, but we have the sense to know it. I don't say she wouldn't be happy—

in a way—as long as the desire lasted. Then she'd leave you—even with the registrar's signature. I'm sorry for you, being mixed up like that, with one of us.

MICHAEL: I'll risk it.

JAMES: And your wife?

MICHAEL: A hysteric will go on with a scene until she gets what she wants. There are only two things you can do. Give her what she wants, and that brings the next scene closer—she smells success, like a dog a bitch. Or just walk out. She can't make a scene alone. I've walked out for half hours long enough. I shall walk out for good. Father, I sound cruel. I'm not. I do love her. She's my wife. She ruined her health over the child. I want to make her happy. I've tried to, but I can't go on. It's no good going on—for any of us. We'll break sooner or later, and it only prolongs the pain. What's the matter? (*He goes over to the chair.*)

    JAMES *is trembling. His head has dropped.*

JAMES: It's a terrible world.

MICHAEL: Can't you forget you're a priest for a while?

JAMES (*with bitter self-reproach*): I forget it twenty-two hours a day.

MICHAEL: As a man, can you see Rose happy in this house—three old people and all these closed rooms? Why closed?

JAMES (*in a low, ashamed voice*): They were afraid to live where anyone had died. So they closed the bedrooms.

MICHAEL (*too patly*): So that's it. I've come across cases like that. Compulsive neurosis. People who won't grow up so that they believe they won't die.

JAMES: How you love your snap judgments, Dennis.

MICHAEL: What a household for Rose. What's going to happen when one of them dies—or you die? Can you see her helping to shift the furniture into another hiding place? Is that the life for a girl?

JAMES: You've got plenty of reason on your side, but—

    A pause.

MICHAEL (*he has a sense of victory*): But what?

JAMES: God has plenty of mercy.

MICHAEL: You can't expect me to depend on that.

JAMES: I don't know that *we* do, often.

MICHAEL: It's no good asking your sister. But I ask you. Let me speak to her.

JAMES: Can't you let her alone for a little to make up her own mind?

MICHAEL: Or your sister to make it up for her?

JAMES (*his last appeal*): You're a psychologist. You know how often young girls fall in love with a man your age, looking for a father.

MICHAEL (*defensively*): What of it?

JAMES: Rose never knew her father.

> *He has got under* MICHAEL'S *skin. His reaction is unnecessarily vehement.*

MICHAEL: All right. I may be a father substitute. I don't care a damn, if it makes her happy. It's as good a reason for love, isn't it, as black hair or a good profile? Hair alters, a man grows a second chin. A substitute may give satisfaction for a lifetime.

JAMES: You can't think in terms of a lifetime.

MICHAEL: I might die before she got tired of me.

JAMES: You might. It's a terrible thing to have to depend on, though.

> *A bell rings below.*

MICHAEL: Can I go and find her?

JAMES: She's not in the house. Helen saw to that.

MICHAEL: Can I wait till she returns?

JAMES: I can't turn you out, can I?

MICHAEL (*he hears footsteps on the stairs*): That's Rose.

JAMES: It's only Mary.

MICHAEL: No. I know her step. She's coming up. Am I going to see her with your consent? Or without?

JAMES: What are you going to say to her?

MICHAEL: I'm going to ask her to pack her bag.

ROSE *enters. She sees* MICHAEL *with surprise and pleasure.*

ROSE: But you telephoned. They said you'd telephoned.

MICHAEL: What about?

ROSE: You couldn't come. You had to go away. For a week.

MICHAEL: I never telephoned. They didn't want me to see you.

ROSE: But that's absurd. Uncle—you weren't concerned?

JAMES: No. He wants to talk to you. You can push me out.

ROSE (*looking from one to the other*): What's happened? What's it all about? You, both of you . . .

JAMES: He wants you to pack your bag.

ROSE (*to* MICHAEL): You mean—go away? They know all about us? Do you want me to go away now, today? (*She speaks with excitement and no apprehension.*)

MICHAEL *watches her with growing uneasiness. She is too young and unprepared.*

How lucky I never unpacked the trunk. I can be ready in a few minutes. (*She turns to her uncle with sudden remorse.*) Oh, Uncle, you must think we are very wicked.

JAMES: No. Just ignorant. And innocent.

ROSE (*with pride*): Not innocent.

JAMES: Please open the door, Rose.

ROSE: I didn't want to hurt you. It just happened this way.

JAMES: Don't worry about *me*.

ROSE: I know it's wrong, but I don't care. Uncle, we're going to be happy.

JAMES: Is he?

ROSE *looks quickly at* MICHAEL. *He doesn't look a happy man.*

ROSE: Darling, is anything the matter?

MICHAEL: My wife knows.

ROSE (*with the glibness and unfeelingness of youth*): It had to happen sooner or later. Was she very angry?

MICHAEL: Not exactly angry.

ROSE: You've had an awful time.

MICHAEL: Other people are having an awful time.

ROSE: Yes, of course. It's terribly sad, but we'll be all right. You'll see. And people get over everything.

MICHAEL: She cried a great deal. I left her crying.

JAMES: Please open the door. I feel like an accomplice.

ROSE: I'm sorry, Uncle. (*She opens the door for his chair to pass.*)

JAMES: Come and see me when you've done.

ROSE: You don't think I'd go away without saying good-bye?

> *Turning to* MICHAEL *after shutting the door.*

Darling, tell me what you've planned.

MICHAEL: My plans haven't been a success. My wife won't divorce me. We may never be able to marry.

ROSE (*with momentary disappointment*): Oh! (*She sweeps her disappointment aside.*) It doesn't really matter, does it? It wouldn't have been a real marriage, anyway. And—somebody may die.

MICHAEL: You're a Catholic. I never knew any Catholics before—except your mother.

ROSE: Perhaps I'm only half one. Father wasn't.

MICHAEL: You never knew him, did you?

ROSE: No. But I've seen lots of photographs. He had a nose rather like yours.

MICHAEL (*with bitterness*): I never noticed that.

ROSE: Shall I pack now?

> *She begins to get her things together in a small suitcase while the dialogue continues.*

MICHAEL: You don't mind—about the Church?

ROSE (*lightly as she goes to the bathroom for her spongebag and pyjamas.*) Oh, I expect it will come all right in the end.

I shall make a deathbed confession and die in the odour of sanctity.

MICHAEL (*as she comes out again*): Our children will be illegitimate.

ROSE: Bastards are the best, so Shakespeare says.

She folds up the pyjamas and puts them in her case.

We did *King John* my last term at school. The nuns hurried over those bits. There was a nice phrase for bastards—'born under the rose'. I liked Faulconbridge. Oh, what an age ago it seems——

MICHAEL: Your aunts won't let you come back here.

ROSE (*crossing to a cupboard to fetch a frock*): Do you think I care? Darling, I can't bear this house. It gives me the creeps. Do you know why they've closed the rooms?

MICHAEL: Yes.

ROSE: I can't help wondering which of them will die where. If one of them died in here, they wouldn't have enough rooms to live in. It's really awful. Like something in Edgar Allen Poe.

MICHAEL: What a lot of books you've read.

ROSE: You aren't angry, about something, are you? I'll do anything you say. Just tell me where to go, and I'll go. Like Ruth. 'Your people shall be my people.' I suppose your people are all psychologists.

MICHAEL: Not all.

ROSE: I've read Freud in Penguin. *The Psychology of Everyday Life.*

MICHAEL: You have, have you?

ROSE: Darling, something's fretting you. You haven't fallen in love with another woman?

MICHAEL: No. I finished all that with you.

ROSE: I shall never be sure of that. You didn't waste much time with me.

MICHAEL: I haven't much time to waste.

ROSE: You are worrying, just like yesterday. What *is* the matter?

MICHAEL: Only a damned sense of responsibility. Listen, Rose, this is serious. Have you really *thought* . . .?

ROSE: I don't *want* to think. You *know* about things, I don't. Darling, I've never been in love before. You have.

MICHAEL: Have I?

ROSE: Your wife.

MICHAEL: Oh, yes.

ROSE: You know the way around. Tell me what to do. I'll do it. I've packed my bag, but I'll unpack it if you want it a different way. I'll do anything, darling, that's easier for you. Tell me to come to Regal Court, now, this minute, and I'll come.

MICHAEL: Regal Court?

ROSE: It's where people go to make love. So everybody says. I'll go there now and come back here. I'll meet you there every day. Or I'll take my bag and go away with you— for years.

MICHAEL: Only years?

ROSE: Just say what you want. I'm awfully obedient.

MICHAEL: Dear, it's not only you and me . . . you have to think.

ROSE: Don't *make* me think. I warned you not to make me think. I don't know about things. They'll all get at me if they have a chance. They'll say, 'Did you ever consider this? Did you ever consider that?' Please don't do that to me too—not yet. Just tell me what to do.

MICHAEL: You are very dear to me.

ROSE: Of course. I know.

MICHAEL: I don't want you to make a mistake.

ROSE: A mistake wouldn't matter so much. There's plenty of time . . .

MICHAEL: 'You're not a cruel man' your uncle said to me. I don't know much about the young. I've caused a lot of trouble in the last few weeks, breaking in . . .

ROSE: And haven't I? Dear, don't worry so. Worries bring worries, my nurse used to say. Let's both give up thinking for a month, and then it will be too late.

MICHAEL: I wish I could.

ROSE: But you can.

MICHAEL: You can live in the moment because the past is so small and the future so vast. I've got a small future, I can easily imagine—even your uncle can imagine it for me. And the past is a very long time and full of things to remember.

ROSE: You weren't so horribly wise yesterday.

MICHAEL: Put up with my 'wisdom'.

ROSE: Of course. If I have to. (*Shutting her case.*) Shall we go?

MICHAEL: I have to go home first—and say good-bye.

ROSE: That's hard for you.

MICHAEL (*harshly*): Don't waste your sympathy on me. After all these years she had the right to feel secure.

ROSE: I'm sorry.

MICHAEL: Oh, it's not you I'm angry with. I'm angry with all the world who think one doesn't care . . .

ROSE: You won't let her talk you round, will you?

MICHAEL: No.

ROSE: She's had you so long. She'll have all the right words to use. I only know the wrong ones.

MICHAEL: You don't need words. You're young. And the young always win in the end. (*He draws her to him.*)

ROSE: Where shall we meet?

MICHAEL: Lancaster Gate Station, in an hour.

ROSE (*she is worried by his reserve*): You do still want me?

MICHAEL: Yes.

ROSE: I mean, like yesterday?

MICHAEL: I still want you in just the same way.

ROSE: I wasn't much good, but I'm learning awfully fast.

MICHAEL: You've nothing to fear. (*He kisses her.*) You've got the whole future.

ROSE: I only want one as long as yours.

MICHAEL (*going*): In an hour.

ROSE: Good-bye, my heart!

> MICHAEL *goes.*
>
> ROSE *closes her suitcase, then goes to the window. She tries to peer out between the bars, then climbs on a chair to see better.* TERESA *enters and crosses the room to the bathroom. As the door closes* HELEN *comes in, sees the suitcase and stops.* ROSE *turns.*

HELEN: I hope you are not opening the window, dear?

ROSE (*obeying*): I'm sorry, Aunt Helen. (*She crosses the room and picks up her suitcase.*)

HELEN: Where are you going?

ROSE: To say good-bye to Uncle James.

> HELEN *sits down heavily in a chair.*

It was very wrong of you to tell me Michael had gone away. I nearly missed him. I'll be back to say good-bye to Aunt Teresa.

> *She goes out.*
>
> HELEN *sits silent in the chair. She puts her fingers to the corners of her eyes and gets rid of the few tears that have formed.*
>
> TERESA *opens the closet door and comes out.*

HELEN (*imperiously*): Teresa! She's going away. We've got to stop her.

> TERESA *pays her no attention and tries to cross the room.* HELEN *bars her way.*

Oh, don't be absurd, Teresa. Don't keep up your tomfoolery now.

> TERESA *evades her and goes out.*

Teresa!

> *After a moment* TERESA *re-enters.*

TERESA: Did you call me, Helen?

HELEN: You heard what I said—(*a sudden doubt*)—or didn't you?

TERESA: I've been in James's room. How could I hear?

HELEN (*furiously*): You've been there—(*pointing at the closet*) —pretending not to be seen again.

TERESA: Oh no, dear, you're imagining things.

HELEN: Do you really mean to tell me . . . Are you feeling quite well, Teresa?

TERESA: I think so, Helen. Was there something you wanted to talk to me about?

HELEN: Sit down, Teresa. You know when you came in just now, you walked a little crookedly. Like ten years ago when the doctor said . . .

TERESA (*in fear*): I don't remember what he said.

HELEN: He said you had to be very, very careful.

TERESA (*whimpering*): I have been, Helen.

HELEN: He said . . .

TERESA (*imploring*): I don't want to hear. I don't want to hear.

HELEN: Shall I read you some of the 'Little Flower?'

TERESA: But you only do that when I'm ill, Helen. Am I ill? Really ill? (*She sits down.*)

HELEN (*sits beside her*): Did you feel a little faint when you got up?

TERESA *licks her lips a little with apprehension.*

TERESA: Perhaps, Helen. For a while.

HELEN: Any headache, dear?

TERESA: I don't think so. A very little one.

HELEN: And your heart?

TERESA: It's beating rather. Helen, you don't think . . .?

HELEN: Of course not. But we have to be very careful at our age. You'll go to bed, dear, won't you?

TERESA: But I don't want to be a trouble, Helen. It's my cooking day tomorrow. There's no one to help you in the evening when Mary leaves.

HELEN: There's Rose now, dear. Rose would help, wouldn't she? She's a good child. She wouldn't leave us if she knew we were in trouble. I'll call her now and we'll put you to bed.

TERESA: But Helen, I hate my bed. Couldn't I just rest in here?

HELEN (*lowering her voice*): But you remember our agreement?

TERESA: I can't hear what you are saying, dear.

HELEN: You seem a little deaf this morning. Your hearing comes and goes. See if you can stand up, Teresa.

TERESA: Of course I can stand up. (*She gets to her feet with difficulty and collapses again in her chair.*)

HELEN: Come to bed, dear. Rose and I will look after you.

TERESA (*imploringly*): Please, Helen . . .

HELEN: You've got such a pretty bedroom, dear. I tell you what. I'll send Mary to Burns Oates to get you another holy picture for that patch on the wall where Mother's portrait used to hang. Would you like another 'Little Flower?'

TERESA: I'd rather have St. Vincent de Paul. But Helen . . .

HELEN: In a few days you'll be up and about again.

TERESA (*desolately*): Days?

HELEN: Come, dear. You'll see you can't walk by yourself. Try.

TERESA: I can. I really can. (*She rises carefully to her feet and takes a step.*)

HELEN: Careful, dear. Take my arm.

TERESA: No. No.

    With a frightened cry TERESA *draws away and collapses on to a chair.* HELEN *goes to the door and calls "Rose! Rose!" It isn't real fear in her voice.* TERESA *takes some tottering steps towards the sofa and falls on the floor. When* HELEN *turns and sees her sister, she feels panic.*

HELEN: Teresa. Dear Teresa. Speak to me. Please. Teresa!

    She bends down and for a moment it looks as though she is

going to try to drag her sister through the door. Then she runs through the door on to the landing and cries in real fear.

Rose! Rose! Please Rose! Help me, Rose! Help me!

CURTAIN

END OF ACT I

ACT II

SCENE I

The living room. Early evening, three weeks later.

TERESA BROWNE *is sitting in an easy chair with a rug tucked round her knees.* FATHER BROWNE *sits beside her in his wheeled chair. He is reading aloud to her.*

JAMES (*reading*):

Upon that lucky night
In secrecy, inscrutable to sight,
I went without discerning
And with no other light
Except for that which in my heart was burning.

It lit and led me through
More certain than the light of noonday clear
To where One waited near
Whose presence well I knew,
There where no other presence might appear.

Oh night that was my guide!
Oh darkness dearer than the morning's pride.

JAMES suddenly stops.

TERESA: Go on a little longer. I like what you read so much better than what Helen reads. I don't understand it, but I like it. She always reads me St. Therese. She talks about *my* 'Little Flower', but it's her 'Little Flower' really.

JAMES: Helen gets confused. She thinks of us two as the old ones, but she's old too. She means no harm.

TERESA: Was I really dying the other day?

JAMES: How do I know? We are all nearly dying I hope—except Rose.

38

TERESA: Do you know for just a moment I didn't want to die in the day nursery where all our toys used to be. I wanted to die where everybody else had died—in a real bedroom.

JAMES: Why not?

TERESA: Oh, it was only for a moment. Then I was so frightened. More frightened than I had ever been. Helen says it was my idea first—to close all the bedrooms. I can't remember. Was it?

JAMES: You both wanted it, I think. I can't remember now. Anyway the rooms will be opened by somebody else before very long—perhaps by Rose.

TERESA: People talk about the soul, but I always think of ghosts, the dead who can't sleep. There was a story Helen told me once about lost souls . . .

JAMES (interrupting): It was wrong of me to give way about those rooms. When it began it seemed silly and unimportant. Why should I fight you over a fancy? But perhaps I should have fought you. I've been very useless, Teresa. Do you know one of my 'day-dreams'? I get them again now—perhaps they belong to second childhood. I dream of helping somebody in great trouble. Saying the right word at the right time. In the old days in the confessional—once in five years perhaps—one sometimes felt one had done just that. It made the years between worth while. Now I doubt if I'd know the right word if the chance came.

TERESA: I'm afraid of dying, James, even of thinking about death. Then Rose came, and I seemed to frighten her. It's a nice house. We aren't bad people. I don't know why there should be so much fear around.

JAMES: Perhaps your fear frightened her. Your silly fear of death.

TERESA: Is it a silly fear, James?

JAMES: No one who believes in God should be afraid of death.

TERESA: But there's Hell, James.

JAMES: We aren't as important as that, Teresa. Mercy is what I believe in. Hell is for the great, the very great. I don't know anyone who's great enough for Hell except Satan.

TERESA: I sound a bit braver now, but it's only because I'm back here—in the living room. It was good of Helen to hide that patch in my room with a picture, but I said *not* the 'Little Flower'. Do you think Helen likes her because she died young? Sometimes she looks at Rose in a strange way, as though she's thinking, I *may* survive even you.

JAMES: You want to rest. Shall I read a little more?

TERESA: Yes.

JAMES: St. John is still talking about the dark night of the soul. It's a bit difficult to understand for me and you who've not got that far. You see it's nearness to God that withers a man up. We are all such a long comfortable distance away. He is trying to describe the black night he found himself in—a night that seemed to be without love or even the power to pray.

TERESA: I pray. Night and morning.

JAMES: Oh, I remember my baby prayers, Teresa. Our Father, Hail Mary, an act of contrition. But I can't meditate for ten minutes without my mind wandering—and as for contemplation it's a whole world away. Something I have read about in the lives of the saints. When I was working in a parish I used to tell myself I had no time for prayer. Well, I have been given twenty years and I can still only say Our Father. And do I really say that?

TERESA: I think you have got a dark night of your own, James.

JAMES: No, I'd never reach that kind of despair. I have no parish drudgery, I'm comfortable, well fed, happy with both of you. I can read you what the saints say from books, even though I can't feel with them. What's for dinner, Teresa?

TERESA: Macaroni cheese. (*Suddenly realising he is joking.*) Oh, James . . .

HELEN *enters*.

HELEN: Have you heard Mary come back, dear?

JAMES: Isn't she in the kitchen?

HELEN: I sent her on an errand.

JAMES: To the shops?

HELEN: Not exactly.

JAMES: Far?

HELEN (*ambiguously*): Oh, across the park.

TERESA: I haven't seen her since lunch.

HELEN: She went out just after lunch. I hoped she'd be back to wash up the tea things, but I suppose I'd better do them myself.

TERESA: Rose?

HELEN: You don't expect Rose to be here, do you, dear?

She goes out.

TERESA: What did she mean?

JAMES: I don't know.

TERESA: Rose was very good to me when I was ill. I'd wake up sometimes so frightened and there she'd be, dozing in the chair by my bed. I remember when I was a child, before Helen was born, Mother used to give me a nightlight because I was so afraid. It made a sound like someone breathing quietly. Like Rose asleep.

JAMES: She's a kind child.

TERESA: Except at the beginning. She was very harsh to me at the beginning. I wonder why.

JAMES: It doesn't matter now.

TERESA: Just before I was ill, I remember Helen saying something to me about Rose going away. Where would she go to? Running away, I think she said. But why should she run away from us? Is that fear again?

JAMES: Don't worry. She's still here.

TERESA: People don't tell me things. And there's such a lot I don't understand.

JAMES: Don't try. It's much better to believe only what we

see, and not ask questions. Leave questions to the psychologists.
'Is this really so?' they ask you. 'Do you really think that or
just think that you think' .

THEY *neither of them have heard the footsteps on the stairs.*
MARY (*outside*): But, Miss Rose . . . Please, Miss Rose.
ROSE: Come along in here.
MARY: I had my orders, Miss Rose.
ROSE: I know what your orders were.

The door is flung open and ROSE *pushes* MARY *in ahead of
her.* ROSE *has changed since we last saw her. She is angry now,
but it isn't that. Three weeks ago she was a muddled, enthusiastic,
excitable child. She looks several years older now. She isn't quite
as pretty as she was. Disappointments, decisions and frustrations
have filled the weeks and she has had time to think. Perhaps
that's the biggest change.*

ROSE: Go on. Tell your story.
MARY: But, Miss Rose . . .
ROSE: Oh, your employer isn't here, is she? (*She goes to the
door and calls out.*) Aunt Helen! Aunt Helen!
TERESA: She's in the kitchen, Rose.
ROSE: She'll be up soon. Now her spy's returned.
MARY: Please, Miss Rose . . .
ROSE: Were you all in on this?
JAMES: We don't even know what *this* is.
ROSE: I'm sorry. I might have guessed it was *her* work.
She hates me.
JAMES: Nonsense.
ROSE: And I know why. Love is normal. Love is being
born and growing older and having children and dying. She
can't bear that. She wants to build a wall of closed rooms—
and in the middle there's this *living* room. Nobody will ever
die here. Perpetual motion. Nobody will ever be born here.
That's risky. I can camp here all night because I'm young and
there's no danger, but a man mustn't come and see me here
because life might not stand still. We might make love and

that means getting older, running risks—in your precious
museum piece of a room. Period 1902.

HELEN *has entered during the last line.*

HELEN: What's that about 1902, little sweet——? (*She sees*
MARY.) Mary, what are you doing here?

ROSE: I brought her up with me. I wanted to hear her
report too.

HELEN: What report, dear?

ROSE: The report on my movements, of course. How I
arrived at Regal Court at two-forty-five and left at five-fifteen.
How she recognised no one else who entered—because he'd
got there first.

HELEN: Mary, you'd better go.

ROSE: I want to hear the report.

HELEN: Go, Mary.

MARY *leaves.*

A pause.

I can't think what you are talking about.

ROSE: Oh yes, you can. And now I'll give you all the details
Mary doesn't know. Michael was there at half-past two—
before me and Mary. I got there at three and I dressed again
at five. She couldn't tell you that, could she? And we didn't
make love all that time. Because people can't. And we'd been
there three or four times every week for three weeks. Ever
since you stopped my running away for good. (*Bitterly.*) With
your great need of help. You could have done without me all
right—if Mary's time had not been taken up this way.

JAMES: Is it true, Helen?

HELEN: Oh, yes, it's true—in a way. I wanted to know
where she went off to nearly every afternoon. I suspected
this.

JAMES: Why?

TERESA *has been quietly crying.*

HELEN: Stop snivelling, Teresa.

JAMES: I said why?

43

HELEN: She's our responsibility. It was my duty to clear this thing up. You're so weak, you threw them together. She told you she was going away with him. It's a mortal sin.

JAMES: How do you know?

HELEN: Because he's a married man, of course.

JAMES: Do you think you know a mortal sin when you see it? You're wiser than the Church then.

HELEN: Have some common sense.

JAMES: Yes: if you would have some charity.

HELEN: James, you're a fool.

JAMES: I see what's in front of my eyes. God doesn't require me to do more—

HELEN: You've heard her—bragging. They'd have been living together now, day in day out, if I hadn't stopped them.

JAMES (*sharply*): Stopped them?

ROSE: Of course we'd have been together. Of course we'd have been lovers. Oh, you talk a lot about mortal sin. Why didn't you let me go? Is this any better? Afternoons at Regal Court.

HELEN: It *is* better. It will soon come to an end—this way.

ROSE: Love ending is a good thing, isn't it? To you.

HELEN: This sort of love.

ROSE: What's the difference between this sort of love and any other? Would making love feel any different if he hadn't got a wife? (*She answers her own question in a lower voice.*) Only happier.

JAMES (*who has been waiting his opportunity*): You said you stopped them?

HELEN: Yes. I'm not ashamed of it. I've kept her in the Church, haven't I? She can go to confession now any time she likes.

ROSE: And do it again, and go to confession, and do it again? Do you call that better than having children, living together till we die . . .

HELEN: In mortal sin.

ROSE: God's got more sense. And mercy.

HELEN: And it's another sin to trust too much to His mercy.

ROSE: Oh, they have a name for that too. I know it. The nuns taught it me. It's called presumption. Well, I'm damned well going to presume.

JAMES (to HELEN): What do you mean, you stopped them?

HELEN: Teresa wasn't ill.

ROSE: Not ill? She was in a faint on the floor.

HELEN: I told her she was ill. She believed it.

ROSE (turning quietly away): Oh.

　　A long silence.

HELEN (defensively): I had to act quickly, James.

JAMES: I'd think you were a very wicked woman if you weren't such a fool.

TERESA: I don't understand what you are all talking about.

JAMES (to HELEN, bitterly): Perhaps *you* can explain it to her, *I* can't. Teresa, dear, go to your room with Helen. You've been up long enough.

TERESA: Are you trying to get rid of me, James?

JAMES: Yes, dear, I am. Take my book. I want a word with Rose alone.

　　TERESA *begins to cross the room. Near the door she pauses.*

TERESA: Aren't you coming, Helen?

HELEN (to JAMES): I don't trust you. I'm staying.

JAMES: If you want to, you will. I know that. Rose, *you* see Teresa to her room.

　　ROSE *takes* TERESA *by the arm and leads her through the door.*

TERESA (as she goes, with a note of appeal, like a child): You'll come and say good-night, James?

JAMES: It's early. I'll come and read to you till you feel sleepy. I'll come before dinner.

　　ROSE *and* TERESA *go out*

JAMES (to HELEN): You might have killed Teresa.

HELEN: I only told her she didn't look well. I'd no intention . . .

JAMES: You've told us clearly enough what you intended.

HELEN: I wish the girl had never come here.

JAMES: Oh, so do I, so do I. We've ruined her between us.

HELEN: Us? We aren't to blame. That man with all his wickedness . . .

JAMES: Don't blame him. Blame our dead goodness. Holy books, holy pictures, a subscription to the Altar Society. Do you think, if she had come into a house where there was love, she wouldn't have hesitated, thought twice, talked to us . . .

HELEN: And why didn't she?

JAMES: Because there was fear, not love, in this house. If we had asked her for a sacrifice, what would we have offered? Pious platitudes.

HELEN: Speak for yourself, James.

JAMES: I do. Goodness that sits and talks piously and decays all the time.

HELEN: He seduced her.

JAMES: It's a silly word, but what if he did? God sometimes diverts the act, but the pious talk He seems to leave like the tares, useless.

ROSE *enters.*

ROSE (*defiantly*): Well?

JAMES (*to* HELEN): You'd better apologise to her.

HELEN: Apologise?

JAMES (*to* ROSE): She had no right to have you followed.

HELEN: She's in our care. She lied to us.

ROSE: You lied to me.

HELEN: There are lies and lies.

JAMES: There needn't be any more. God forgive me, but you bore me, Helen. Please go away.

HELEN: I'm going to stay here.

JAMES: I know I'm your brother, but I'm still a priest. I've asked you to go.

HELEN *makes for the door, but she flings back one more insult.*

46

HELEN: Oh, the Church is well rid of a useless priest like you, James.

>*She goes and the door closes.*
>*Silence.*

ROSE (*defiantly*): You know what this means? (*No answer.*) If Aunt Teresa's well, I'm free. I can go with him. We are just where we were.

JAMES: Are you?

ROSE: We haven't tired of each other, if that's what you mean. (*Defiantly.*) We love each other more. We know each other properly now.

JAMES: I'm glad the hours in Regal Court were so rewarding.

ROSE (*her voice breaking*): Don't laugh at me. Please don't laugh at me.

JAMES: I don't feel like laughing.

ROSE: Uncle, it isn't wonderful at all. It's sad, sad. (*Sitting on the floor by his chair.*) I'm tired. I don't know what to do.

JAMES: How is he standing it?

ROSE: We both stand it when we are together. We are happy at half-past two, we are still happy at three o'clock. Then we sometimes sleep a bit. It's not so bad at four o'clock, but then we hear the quarter strike and all the sadness starts. Every day at a quarter-past four. We behave awfully sensibly when five o'clock comes. There's a beastly little French gilt clock on the mantelpiece. One day I'm going to smash its pretty face. I oughtn't to tell you all this.

JAMES: I want to hear. People don't talk to priests much—except in formulas, in that coffin-shaped box of ours.

ROSE: 'Since my last confession three weeks ago I've committed adultery twenty-seven times.' That's what Aunt Helen would like me to say, and, Father, it doesn't mean a thing. We are supposed to be talking to God, aren't we, through you, and God knows all about the clock on the mantelpiece. I don't want to confess. I want to say, 'Dear God. Give us more love.

Give us a life together. Don't let it be just Regal Court over and over again.' Do you understand?

JAMES: A little. All I can.

ROSE: What are we to do?

JAMES: My dear . . .

ROSE (*interrupting him*): I'm not asking you as a priest, I know *that* answer. But I can't believe it's true what Aunt Helen says, that God would rather have Regal Court and saying good-bye three times a week than—the other thing.

JAMES: What?

ROSE: Oh, peace and children and getting older. Outside the Church.

JAMES: You wouldn t be happy . . .

ROSE: Oh yes, I would. Don't make any mistake about that, Father. I could live a lifetime without the sacraments. That wouldn't hurt—but a lifetime, without him . . .

JAMES: One gets over a separation. Time passes.

ROSE: You have to live through it first though. You have to dream at night you are together and wake up in the morning alone, and count the hours till bed again.

JAMES (*sadly and with amazement*): What a lot of growing up you've done in three weeks.

ROSE: Do you think if I left Michael I could really love a God who demanded all that pain before He'd give Himself . . .

JAMES: You simplify too much.

ROSE: But it's a simple situation, Father. There's nothing complicated about this—love affair. I'm not a case history.

JAMES: The trouble is you don't trust God enough. He would make things so much easier for you if you would shut your eyes and leave it to Him.

> ROSE'S *face hardens during this speech. She will not be persuaded.*

ROSE: Would He? It's not the way He always works. Look round the world nowadays. He seems to want heroes and I'm not a hero. I'm a coward. I can't bear too much pain.

There are a lot of us like that, Father. When I betray Him,
I'm not doing any worse than Peter, am I? God died for the
cowards too.

> *A bell rings below.*

JAMES: He made them into heroes, even Peter.

ROSE: Oh, we read about God's successes. We don't read
about His failures. His happy failures. Who just don't care
much about Him, and go on living quietly all the same.

JAMES: One has to deserve to be a failure.

ROSE: But, Uncle, I don't want to try, I'm a coward. I just
want a bit of ordinary human comfort. Not formulas. 'Love
God. Trust God. Everything will be all right one day.'
Uncle, please say something that's not Catholic.

> HELEN *enters hurriedly.*

HELEN: There's someone downstairs to see you, Rose.

JAMES: Who?

HELEN: Mrs. Dennis.

JAMES: What does she want? (*With suspicion.*) Who brought
her here?

HELEN (*with a suspicion of secret triumph*): I've told you—she
wants to see Rose.

> ROSE *turns away with a movement of panic.*
>
> *A pause.*

JAMES: Is this your work again, Helen? Tell her Rose is
sick, not here. Tell her anything, but get rid of her.

HELEN: She has a right . . .

JAMES: This child has had enough to stand.

HELEN (*scornfully*): Child?

JAMES: Yes. Child.

> ROSE *suddenly turns back to them.*

ROSE: I'm here, aren't I? What are you waiting for? Tell
her to come up. (*She crosses to the door and pulls it open.* HELEN
passes quickly through and is heard calling to MARY *to show* MRS.
DENNIS *up.*)

JAMES (*unwilling to go*): Can you stand it?

49

ROSE: I've been standing the thought of her, haven't I, all these weeks.

JAMES stops his chair by the door and appeals again.

JAMES: Call me if you need me. I'll be in my room.

ROSE obstinately makes no reply and JAMES leaves.

ROSE stands alone, facing the door as MARY shows MRS. DENNIS in and hurriedly closes the door on her. MRS. DENNIS is a woman of about forty-five, with prematurely grey hair and a strained neurotic but determined face. She comes in and looks uneasily about her as though the strangeness of this living room communicated itself even to her.

MRS. DENNIS: Is Michael here?

ROSE: No. Did you expect him to be?

MRS. DENNIS: He said he was at a lecture, but I never know now. You're Rose, aren't you?

ROSE: You're his wife, aren't you?

MRS. DENNIS: I read one of your letters. It fell out of his dressing-gown pocket.

ROSE: Yes?

MRS. DENNIS: He's always been silly that way—keeping letters.

ROSE: Is that what you've come to tell me? Was it worth climbing all those stairs?

MRS. DENNIS (*maliciously*): I thought your letter so touching. You trust him so much.

ROSE: Yes. I do.

MRS. DENNIS: You shouldn't, you know, but of course you can't know, he wouldn't tell you. But there's always been trouble with his students. Reading Freud together, I suppose. The third year we were married—just after our baby died—I could have divorced him.

ROSE: Why didn't you?

MRS. DENNIS (*fiercely*): Because he's happier with me. He'll always be happier with me. I'd forgive him anything. Would **you**?

ROSE: No. Because I love him. I wouldn't want to hold him prisoner with forgiveness. I wouldn't want to hold him a minute if he wanted to be somewhere else.

MRS. DENNIS: He only *thinks* that.

ROSE: He has a right to think. He has a right to think wrong.

MRS. DENNIS: If he really loved you, he'd have left me.

ROSE: He meant to. Three weeks ago.

MRS. DENNIS: But he's still here.

ROSE: Because I wouldn't go.

MRS. DENNIS: Why?

ROSE: I was caught like him. By pity (*savagely*)—He pities you.

MRS. DENNIS (*maliciously*): It didn't feel like pity—last night.

ROSE (*crying out in pain*): I don't believe you.

MRS. DENNIS: If I'm ready to share him, what right . . .

ROSE: You're lying. You know you are lying. What have you come here for? You're just lying to break me. You're wicked.

MRS. DENNIS: Wicked's an odd word from you. I *am* his wife.

ROSE: You can stay his wife. I only want to be his mistress.

> MRS. DENNIS *suddenly crumbles. She drops into a chair and begins to weep.* ROSE *watches her for a moment, but she cannot remain indifferent.*

I'm sorry. (*With a gesture of despair.*) Oh, it's all such a mess.

MRS. DENNIS: Please don't take him away.

ROSE: What can I do? I love him. I love him terribly.

MRS. DENNIS: But I love him too. I only want him near me still. It doesn't hurt you.

ROSE (*bitterly*): Doesn't it?

MRS. DENNIS: I was lying. We haven't—been together like that for years

ROSE: Oh, love isn't all making love. I'd sometimes give that up, to be together. At meals. Come into a house where he is. Sit silent with a book in the same room.

MRS. DENNIS (*hysterically*): When are you going? I know you are planning to go. Don't torture me. Tell me.

ROSE: I don't know.

MRS. DENNIS: You're young. You can find any number of men. Please let him alone. (*Spacing her words.*) I can't live without him.

> ROSE *watches her hysteria grow. She is trapped and horrified.*

I'll die if he leaves me. I'll kill myself.

ROSE: No. No. You never will.

MRS. DENNIS: I will. I know what you're thinking—after that, I could marry him.

ROSE: Please . . .

MRS. DENNIS: Go away from him. Please. Go somewhere he won't find you. You're young. You'll get over it. The young always do.

ROSE: But I don't want to get over it.

MRS. DENNIS: I'm ill. Can't you wait? Just wait six months and see. Six months isn't long. (*With almost a cry.*) You haven't any right to hurt me like this. (*She gets up and comes across the floor to* ROSE.) No right. (*Suddenly she strikes* ROSE *in the face, but immediately she has struck she goes down on her knees and starts beating the table with her fists.*) You made me do that. You made me. I want to die. I want to die. I want to die.

> ROSE *stands helplessly above her as* MRS. DENNIS *beats the table. She doesn't know what to do.*

He wants me to die too. You all want me to die.

ROSE: No. No. (*In a moan of despair.*) We only want to be happy.

MRS. DENNIS: If he runs away, I shall go mad. (*She gets clumsily to her feet. The paroxysm is over. She sits down in a chair again.*) Please will you get me some water?

ROSE *goes to the closet door. As she enters the closet,* MRS. DENNIS *hurriedly gets up and finds her bag which she had laid on the table. A taps runs. She takes a bottle out of her bag and unscrews the top. As* ROSE *comes in again she conceals the bottle in her palm. She takes the glass of water.*

MRS. DENNIS: Could you turn out that light, dear? It's so strong.

ROSE *turns away to find the switch.* MRS. DENNIS *begins to pour some tablets into her hand. She does it slowly with the obvious purpose that she shall be seen when* ROSE *turns. When* ROSE *sees what she is at, she runs to her and snatches the bottle which she throws into a corner of the room.*

(*Hysterically*): Why did you do that? I can buy more.

Rose: Buy them then. You're just blackmailing me.

She hears the sound of feet coming rapidly up the stairs and runs to the door.

Michael, for God's sake. (MICHAEL *enters.*) Michael.

MICHAEL (*looking at his wife*): I heard she was here.

ROSE (*breaking down*): She tried to kill herself.

MICHAEL: Oh no, she didn't. I know that trick of hers. (*To his wife.*) You promised you wouldn't do that again. It does no good, dear.

MRS. DENNIS: Don't call me dear.

MICHAEL: You are dear. I call you what you are.

ROSE *watches. She is distressed, puzzled. She hasn't yet grown up enough to realise that there are many ways of love.*

MRS. DENNIS: But you are going to leave me?

MICHAEL: Yes.

MRS. DENNIS: Oh, you've said it now. You've said it. You've never *said* it before.

MICHAEL: I've been weak. I know. I've made matters worse. I'm supposed to know about people's minds, but when it comes to the point I behave like everyone else.

MRS. DENNIS: She's too young for you, Michael.

MICHAEL (*with bitterness*): I'm making her older already.

MRS. DENNIS: What happens to me, Michael? There isn't even a child.

MICHAEL: You'll settle down. You have friends. After a little while (*he is almost pleading his own cause with her*) surely we can see each other.

> ROSE *turns sharply away. She can't bear any longer the sight of them together. They are unmistakably man and wife.*

MRS. DENNIS: If you go away, you'll never see me again. You won't know what's happening to me. You won't know if I'm ill or well. I'm not going to have you come and watch my tears.

MICHAEL: But I want you to be happy. We haven't been happy. Long before I met Rose . . .

MRS. DENNIS: You talk so much about happiness. No. I wasn't happy. Do you think I'm going to be more happy without you? Happiness isn't everything, is it? Do you often come across someone happy at your lectures? I don't want to be alone, Michael. I'm afraid of being alone. Michael, for God's sake . . . I forgot. You don't believe in God. Only *she* does.

> ROSE *can stand it no more. She comes back into the fight.*

ROSE: Stop. Please stop. You are making it so complicated. Both of you.

> *They both turn and look at her. It's as if she were the outsider. She looks from one to the other.*

We love each other, Mrs. Dennis. It's as simple as that. This happens every day, doesn't it? You read it in the papers. People can't all behave like this. There are four hundred divorces a month.

MICHAEL: Then there are hundreds of suffering people.

ROSE: But, darling, *you* aren't going to suffer, are you? You want to live with me. You want to go away. You don't want to stay with her. We are going to be happy.

MRS. DENNIS: You see—*she* doesn't suffer.

MICHAEL (*turning on her angrily*): She doesn't shout it aloud, that's all. She doesn't use it as a weapon. (*Lowering his voice*.) I'm sorry. I'm shouting too. This is making us all hysterical.

MRS. DENNIS: You won't have to be hysterical any more. (*She gets up*.) You can go home. (*She catches on the word*.) I mean to the house—and pack. I won't be there. I'll keep out of the way till you've gone. (*She walks to the door*.) You can sleep there tonight. I won't be there.

> *She goes.*
>
> ROSE *holds out a hand to* MICHAEL, *but he doesn't see it. He is staring at the door.*

MICHAEL (*to himself*): God knows what she'll do.

> *He leaves the room, and we hear him calling to her from the head of the stairs—it is the first time we have heard her first name.*

(*Outside, calling*): Marion! Marion!

> ROSE *listens with her hand still held out. Then she lets it fall to her side.*

(*Outside*): Marion! (*He comes slowly back into the room—talking more to himself than to* ROSE, *to keep his courage up*.) She won't do anything. People who talk about suicide never do anything.

> *A pause.*

Do they?

ROSE: No. What are *we* going to do, Michael?

> *He doesn't hear her. His eyes are on the door.*

Michael! Michael!

MICHAEL: Yes?

ROSE: What are we going to do, Michael?

MICHAEL (*with unhappy bitterness*): Oh, we are going to be happy.

ROSE: Are *you*?

MICHAEL: Of course. And you. We'll both get over this. (*Still with bitterness against himself*.) It's easy to get over other people's pain. I know. I deal with it all day long. Pain is my profession.

ROSE: Did you mean what you said to her? That we are going away?

MICHAEL: Did I tell her that? Oh yes, she made me angry.

ROSE: Didn't you mean it?

MICHAEL: Of course. As soon as your aunt's better. We always said so.

ROSE: She's better now. I'm free.

MICHAEL (*slowly*): Then—of course—we can go.

ROSE: When? Now? Tomorrow?

> MICHAEL *hesitates very slightly.*

MICHAEL: The day after. You see—I must find out how she is.

ROSE: I wish you didn't love her so.

MICHAEL: My dear, my dear—there's no need of jealousy.

ROSE: I'm not jealous. I hate to see you suffer. That's all.

MICHAEL: We'll be all right—the day after tomorrow. (*He kisses her and goes to the door.*)

ROSE (*anxious, not knowing what to say, in a schoolgirl accent*): A bientôt.

MICHAEL (*his mind still on his wife*): I wish I knew where she'd gone. She hasn't many friends.

> *He goes out.*

> ROSE, *at that last phrase, puts her hand over her mouth. As soon as she hears his feet on the stairs she sits miserably down, her hand still clamped over her mouth, as though that can stop tears. The sound of* HELEN'S *voice and the grind of the chair wheels drives her to her feet.* HELEN *pushes in her brother in his chair.*

HELEN: When are you leaving? It's convenient to know.

ROSE (*the phrase sounds weak even to her*): The day after tomorrow.

HELEN (*to her brother*): Don't forget you've promised to read to Teresa.

JAMES: I won't forget. But there's something you've forgotten.

HELEN *hesitates, then goes to* ROSE *and kisses her cheek.*
HELEN *leaves.*

ROSE *feels the place as though she were feeling a roughness of
the skin. A long pause.*

Can I help at all?

ROSE (*as though to herself*): I told him not to make me think.
I warned him not to.

FATHER BROWNE *sits hunched in his chair saying nothing.*

If we'd gone that day we'd have been happy. I don't think
unless people make me. I can't think about people I don't
know. She was just a name, that's all. And then she comes
here and beats her fists on the table and cries in the chair. I
saw them together. They are *married*, Uncle. I never knew
they were married. Oh, he'd told me they were, but I hadn't
seen them, had I? It was only like something in a book, but
now I've seen them together. I've seen him touch her arm.
Uncle, what am I to do? (*She flings herself on the ground beside
him.*) Tell me what to do, Father!

JAMES: When you say 'Father', you seem to lock my mouth.
There are only hard things to say.

ROSE: I only want somebody to say, 'Do this, do that, I only
want somebody to say, 'Go here, go there.' I don't want to
think any more.

JAMES: And if I say, 'Leave him' . . .

ROSE: I couldn't bear the pain.

JAMES: Then you'd better go with him, if you're as weak as
that.

ROSE: But I can't bear hers, either.

JAMES: You're such a child. You expect too much. In a
case like yours we always have to choose between suffering
our own pain or suffering other people's. We can't *not* suffer.

ROSE: But there *are* happy people. People run away all the
time and are happy. I've read about them.

JAMES: I've read about them too. And the fairy stories
which say, 'They lived happily ever afterwards.'

ROSE: But it *can* be true.

JAMES: Perhaps—for fools. My dear, you're neither of you fools. He spends his time dissecting human motives. He knows his own selfishness, just in the same way as you know your own guilt. A psychologist and a Catholic, you can't fool yourselves—except for two hours in Regal Court.

ROSE: I can. I can.

JAMES: You've got a lifetime to fool yourself in. It's a long time, to keep forgetting that poor hysterical woman who has a right to need him.

ROSE (*crying out with pain*): Oh!

> *The door opens and* TERESA *enters in her dressing-gown.* ROSE, *with her hand over her mouth, follows with her eyes.* TERESA, *paying no attention to them, goes to the closet. As the door closes,* ROSE *sobs on her uncle's knee. He tries to soothe her with his hand. She raises her head.*

It's horrible, horrible, horrible!

JAMES: I hoped you'd go on thinking it was funny.

ROSE: I can't go on living here with them. Like this. In a room where nobody has died. Uncle, please tell me to go. Tell me I'm right to go. Don't give me a *Catholic* reason. Help me. Please help me.

JAMES: I want to help you. I want to be of use. I would want it if it were the last thing in life I could have. But when I talk my tongue is heavy with the Penny Catechism.

ROSE: Can't you give me anything to hope for?

JAMES: Oh, hope! That's a different matter. There's always hope.

ROSE: Hope of what?

JAMES: Of getting over it. Forgetting him.

> ROSE *jumps to her feet and swings away from him. He is struggling for words but can find none—except formulae.*

Dear, there's always the Mass. It's there to help. Your Rosary, you've got a Rosary, haven't you? Perhaps Our Lady . . . prayer.

ROSE (*with hatred and contempt*): Prayer!

JAMES: Rose . . . please . . . (*He is afraid of what she may say and desperately seeking for the right words, but still he can't find them.*) Just wait . . .

ROSE: You tell me if I go with him he'll be unhappy for a lifetime. If I stay here, I'll have nothing but that closet and this—this living room. And you tell me there's hope and I can pray. Who to? Don't talk to me about God or the saints. I don't believe in your God who took away your legs and wants to take away Michael. I don't believe in your Church and your Holy Mother of God. I don't believe. I don't believe.

JAMES holds out a hand to her, but she draws away from it.

I wish to God I didn't feel so lonely.

HELEN enters. She takes the scene coldly in.

HELEN: It's nearly dinner time. Teresa's been asking for you, and I've got to lay the table here.

JAMES: Couldn't we tonight—use another room?

HELEN: You know very well there isn't another room.

She takes his chair and pushes him to the door. He makes no further protest. He feels too old and broken.

(*To* ROSE): If you'll start laying, I'll be with you in a moment.

HELEN pushes JAMES out.

ROSE is alone.

ROSE: I don't believe. I don't believe.

She drags herself across the room. She sees the bottle and kneels down and picks it up. Then desperately she goes towards the closet door and calls.

Aunt Teresa! Dear Aunt Teresa . . .

The closet door opens and TERESA *comes out. She moves across the room, ignoring* ROSE, *as is her custom.*

Please, Aunt Teresa . . .

For a moment the old fuddled brain seems to take in the appeal. She half turns to ROSE, *then walks on to the door.*

For God's sake, speak to me, Aunt Teresa! It's Rose!

> TERESA *goes out and shuts the door behind her.*

> ROSE *sinks hopelessly down on the landing outside the closet door.*

Won't somebody help me?

> *She begins to shake the tablets out of the bottle. When she has them all in her hand, she makes an attempt to pray, but she can't remember the words.*

Our Father who art . . . who art . . .

> *Suddenly she plunges into a childish prayer quite mechanically and without thinking of what she's saying, looking at the tablets in her hand.*

Bless Mother, Nanny and Sister Marie-Louise, and please God don't let school start again ever.

CURTAIN

SCENE II

> *The Living Room. Next morning.*

> *A lot of bedding is piled on the floor.* FATHER JAMES BROWNE *sits in his chair and* MICHAEL DENNIS *has his back turned to him and is staring through the window.* MARY, *the daily woman, is dragging a heavy chair towards the door.*

MARY (*pausing*): 'Miss Helen,' I said, 'it's time you let things rest where they rightly belong.' 'Mary,' she said, 'you are paid by the hour for your services and not for your advice.'

JAMES: Do you want help with that chair?

MARY: I'd rather not, sir. Let each stick to his own job, or more harm's done. (*She gets the chair almost to the door, and turns again. To* JAMES.) I wish I'd said to her, 'Miss Helen, I'm paid for housework,' before ever I went watching that poor girl.

JAMES: There are a terrible lot of vain wishes about the house today.

MARY: I'm forgetting the bedding. (*She piles the bedding on the chair.*) It's an awful waste of space. Will they let me keep the empty trunks in here, do you think? And where will you be eating your meals now? It seems a shame to me in a house as big as this there shouldn't be one living room for all of you.

HELEN *enters during her speech.*

HELEN: You are taking a long time, Mary.

MICHAEL *moves from the window and* HELEN *sees him.*

I didn't know Mr. Dennis was here.

MARY *leaves.*

MICHAEL: I came to see her. You hadn't even the mercy to warn me she was dead.

HELEN: But you're not one of the family. (*She picks up a chair.*)

MICHAEL: For somebody so frightened of death you've done a lot of harm.

HELEN (*carefully ignoring* MICHAEL): James, if we use Teresa's room as a bed-sitting-room—it's large enough—we shan't have to move you at all.

JAMES: I'm not interested today in where I sleep.

HELEN: If you were a woman you'd realise that life has to go on.

MICHAEL: Rose was a woman, and she had a different idea.

HELEN *puts down the chair.*

HELEN: Why are you blaming me for this? If anyone's guilty, it's you. (*To* MICHAEL.) It's you who've been killing her—all these weeks at Regal Court. Killing her conscience, so in the end she did—that.

MICHAEL (*accusingly to* HELEN): If you hadn't brought my wife here, there'd have been no sleeping pills.

JAMES: There would have been a window, a Tube train. It

won't help her to choose who's guilty. (*To* MICHAEL.) And you are not supposed to believe in guilt.

HELEN: I *know* the guilty one.

MICHAEL (*breaking out*): You do, do you. Look in your damned neurotic heart . . .

JAMES: I thought Freud said there was no such thing as guilt . . .

MICHAEL: For God's sake, don't talk psychology at me today. Psychology wasn't any use to her. Books, lectures, analysis of dreams. Oh, I knew the hell of a lot, didn't I, about the human mind—(*Turning away*). She lay on this floor.

JAMES: And our hearts say guilty.

MICHAEL: Yes. Guilty.

HELEN: Mine doesn't.

MICHAEL: Then why don't you sleep in this room? You're innocent. All right then. What are you afraid of?

JAMES: Yes, what are you afraid of, Helen?

HELEN (*startled*): You know we agreed . . .

JAMES: Agreed?

HELEN: I couldn't frighten Teresa like that. You know how she feels. We can't go against Teresa—she's so old. I'm not afraid, but Teresa . . .

JAMES: It's Teresa, is it?

HELEN: Of course it's Teresa. No one should sleep in this room, James.

JAMES: Even me?

HELEN (*fearfully*): It's all decided, James. Teresa's bedroom will be the living room too. Mary's preparing it now. You know what a lovely room it is, James. Plenty of space. (*Puts the chair outside the door and returns.*) It's time to close this room.

JAMES: You can leave us, Helen, and see about your business.

HELEN *hesitates, with her eye on* MICHAEL.

The room won't harm him and me for the little time we'll be here.

HELEN *makes to reply, but instead she picks up a small chair and goes out.*

A pause.

MICHAEL: Three weeks ago Rose and I came into this room together. A lover and his inexperienced mistress. (*As though defending himself.*) You can't believe how happy she was that day.

JAMES: She grew up quickly.

MICHAEL: Did she talk to you last night?

JAMES: Yes.

MICHAEL: Why did she do it?

JAMES: She was afraid of pain. Your pain, her pain, your wife's pain.

MICHAEL: It was my wife who rang me here just now. She'd heard. God knows how. She was—terribly—sympathetic.

JAMES: What will you do?

MICHAEL: Go on living with her. If you can call it living. It's a funny thing. I'm supposed to be a psychologist and I've ruined two people's minds.

JAMES: Psychology may teach you to know a mind. It doesn't teach you to love.

MICHAEL: I did love her.

JAMES: Oh yes, I know. And I thought I loved her too. But none of us loves enough. Perhaps the saints. Perhaps not even them. Dennis, I've got to tell somebody this. You *may* understand. It's your job to understand.

MICHAEL (*bitterly*): My job——.

JAMES: For more than twenty years I've been a useless priest. I had a real vocation for the priesthood—perhaps you'd explain it in terms of a father complex. Never mind now. I'm not laughing at you. To me it was a real vocation. And for twenty years it's been imprisoned in this chair—the desire to help. You have it too in your way, and it would still be there if you lost your sight and speech. Last night God gave me my chance. He flung this child, here, at my knees, asking for help, asking for hope. That's what she said, 'Can't you give me anything to hope for?' I said to God, 'Put words into my mouth,' but he's given me twenty years in this chair with nothing to do but prepare for such a moment, so why should He interfere? And all I said was, 'You can pray.' If I'd ever really known what prayer was, I would only have had to touch her to give her peace. 'Prayer,' she said. She almost spat the word.

MICHAEL: I went away to look for my wife. I was frightened about *her*. What do we do now? Is everything going to be the same as before?

JAMES: Three old people have lost a living room, that's all. A psychologist with a sick wife. She's fallen like a stone into a pond.

MICHAEL: Can you believe in a God who lets that happen?

JAMES: Yes.

MICHAEL: It's a senseless creed.

JAMES: It seems that sometimes.

MICHAEL: And cruel.

JAMES: There's one thing I remember from the seminary. I've forgotten nearly all the things they taught me, even the arguments for the existence of God. It comes from some book of devotion. 'The more our senses are revolted, uncertain and in despair, the more surely Faith says: "This is God: all goes well." '

MICHAEL: 'All goes well.' Do you really feel that?

JAMES: My senses don't feel it. They feel nothing but revolt, uncertainty, despair. But I know it—at the back of my mind. It's my weakness that cries out.

MICHAEL: I can't believe in a God who doesn't pity weakness.

JAMES (*imploringly*): I wish you'd leave Him alone today. Don't talk of Him with such hatred even if you don't believe in Him. If He exists, He loved her too, and saw her take that

senseless drink. And you don't know and I don't know the·
amount of love and pity He's spending on her now.

MICHAEL (*bitterly*): A little late.

JAMES (*pleading*): I wish you could understand that today
it's only your pain speaking. All right, that's natural. Let it
speak. Let it have its silly way. There's a man down the road
dying of cancer. His pain is speaking too. Of course we are in
pain. Do you want to be the only exception in a world of
pain?

MICHAEL: And *you* believe God made the world like that.

JAMES: Yes. And I believe He shared its pain. But He
didn't only make the world—He made eternity. Suffering is a
problem to us, but it doesn't seem a big problem to the woman
when she has borne her child. Death is our child, we have to
go through pain to bear our death. I'm crying out with the
pain like you. But Rose—she's free, she's borne her child.

MICHAEL: You talk as if she were alive. (*Rounding suddenly
on* JAMES.) Oh yes, your Church teaches she's alive all right.
She teaches she's damned—damned with my wife's sleeping
pills.

JAMES: We aren't as stupid as you think us. Nobody claims
we can know what she thought at the end. Only God was with
her at the end.

MICHAEL: You said yourself she almost spat the word
'prayer'.

JAMES: It may not have been her last word, and even if it
were, *you* ought to know you can't tell love from hate some·
times.

MICHAEL: Oh, she wasn't complicated. There was no
neurosis about her. No middle-aged conflicts. She was young
and simple, that's all. And she cared no more about your
Church than I do.

JAMES: Do you really think you'd have loved her if she'd
been as simple as all that? Oh no, you're a man with a vocation
too. You loved the tension in her. Don't shake your head at

me. You loved her just because she was capable of despair. So did I. Some of us are too small to contain that terrible tide— she wasn't, and we loved her for that.

MICHAEL (*bitterly*) : A stone in a pond.

> *The door opens and* TERESA *enters. The old lady is staggering under a load of bedding that she planks down on the sofa.*

JAMES: What is it, Teresa?

TERESA: My room can be the living room. I shall sleep here.

> HELEN'S *voice is heard outside.*

HELEN (*voice outside*): Teresa. Where are you, Teresa?

> HELEN *follows her sister into the room. She is too agitated to pay any attention to* MICHAEL.

HELEN: Teresa, are you ill again? What are you doing? Whose bedding is that? Everything's arranged.

TERESA: I'm sleeping here. (*Begins sorting out the bedding.*)

HELEN: Here? James, tell her she can't. She doesn't understand what she's doing. She can't sleep here. I won't allow her to sleep here. We all agreed. Please, James, say something to her.

> TERESA *continues unperturbed, and* JAMES *watches the two women from his chair while* MICHAEL *turns from the window to watch also.*

(*She is in a panic now.*) Teresa! Dear Teresa! You can't! She died in here. In this room, Teresa!

> HELEN *tries to snatch the clothes off the couch again, kneeling beside it.*

JAMES: Stop it, Helen. We've had enough of this foolishness. God isn't unmerciful like a woman can be. You've been afraid too long. It's time for you to rest, my darling. It's time for you to rest.

> HELEN *collapses suddenly across the bed crying like a child back in the nursery.* TERESA *is the strong one now, she sits beside her, smooths her hair and talks to her in the nursery language of an elder sister.*

66

TERESA: Tears, tears, tears—they are only good to water cabbages. It's all nonsense, my dear. Why shouldn't I sleep here? We're not afraid of the child. And there'd be no better room for me to fall asleep in for ever than the room where Rose died.

She is still comforting HELEN *as the curtain falls.*

CURTAIN

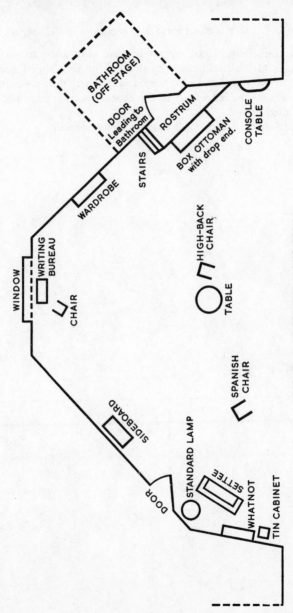

GROUND PLAN FOR THE LIVING ROOM

PROPERTY PLOT

--

ACT I

Settee D.R. with cushions
Lamp standard and shade
Sideboard with blue and white vase, white statuette
Pedestal with large potted palm, above sideboard
Writing desk: on it china bowl, letters, papers, etc.
Upright chair in front of desk
Wardrobe left of desk. In it:
    large piece of cretonne draped to resemble clothes bag
    two slips
    one pair pants
    three pairs of stockings
    one pair of shoes
Box ottoman, D.L. below stairs and rostrum. On it:
    one pillow in case
    one blanket
Spanish chair D.R.
Round table with red chenille cloth, C.
High-backed chair L. table
Console table D.L. On it:
    large china vase
What-not behind settee, with bowls, jugs and vases
Dark red curtains in window.

If the interior of the bathroom is seen, the following should be on view:
Bath
Geyser
Basin

Towel rail

Lavatory pedestal

Bath mat, towels, sponge bag, tumbler, pyjamas hanging on
hook behind door

Personal props:

Wicker work-basket containing wool, several bills

One book—Poems of St. John of the Cross

One suitcase

One copy of *The Lady* magazine

One pair of scissors

One copy of *The Times* newspaper

Brief-case

Small pillow in case

Knitted rug

Small bottle containing 'sleeping pills'.

Wheelchair with dark grey rug, and ashtray on arm.

Tea tray. On it:

    tea pot with tea

    sugar basin with loaf sugar and tongs

    milk jug with milk

    five cups and saucers and spoons

Three-tier cake stand. On it:

    plate of bread and butter (top)

    plate of fruit cake (middle)

Effects:

Bell

Door slam

Property Changes:

ACT I, SCENE I:

    Remove: Cake stand, tea tray, bedding

    Set: Suitcase up stage of Wardrobe. *The Lady*, scissors
        and *The Times* on centre table. Spanish chair slightly
        more up stage

ACT II, SCENE I:

> *Remove:* *The Lady*, scissors and *The Times*
>
> *Set:* High-backed chair to R. of table. Table move a little L. Book of poems on table. Wheelchair L. of ottoman
>
> Reset bedding on ottoman *plus* two sheets

ACT II, SCENE II:

> *Remove:* Sideboard, desk, pedestal and palm, table, settee, lamp standard, curtains, loose cover from ottoman, sleeping pills, vase from console table
>
> *Set:* Spanish chair well down R. High-backed chair down R. Piles of bedding